Glorious Christmas Crafts

A Treasury of Wonderful Creations for the Holiday Season

Anna Hobbs

ISBN-13: 978-1-897330-26-5
ISBN-10: 1-897330-26-X

Produced by
Madison Press Books
1000 Yonge St., Suite 200
Toronto, Ontario
Canada
M4W 2K2

Printed and bound in China.

Contents

Introduction

Christmas is a glorious season — a time when smiles are warmest, people, friendliest and children, wide-eyed with anticipation, capture our hearts. It's a time of treasured memories and fond anticipations, when every year holds the promise of being "the best Christmas ever."

Whatever the ingredients that make the season memorable for you — family, friends, faith, goodwill, music, grandma's cooking, laughter and, of course, lots of surprises — at the heart of Christmas are love and joy.

This book was written for those who love Christmas and have discovered the special joy in adding their own personal touch to holiday preparations and gifts. There are imaginative ideas for decorating your home and trimming your tree; for making the gift you can hardly wait to give; planning a bang-up bazaar; and keeping little hands out of mischief at the busiest time of the year.

From beginner to expert, there's something here for everyone — from jolly paper Santas that can be turned out in minutes by the kindergarten crowd to a breathtaking treetop angel to inspire an experienced needleworker. You'll find adorable dolls and toys to light up the faces of small members of the family — as well as things they can make, too. Many of the ideas here are more-love-than-money crafts made with materials you already have around the house. There are projects to embroider, knit, stitch, quilt, cut and paste, carve from wood and paint. Some need to be kept a secret while hidden under construction for weeks. Others can be whipped up at a moment's notice.

Full-color photographs accompany each project. The instructions are written in an easy-to-follow, step-by-step format, with a complete list of supplies needed. You will find these instructions concise yet detailed enough to leave no unanswered questions. Seventeen patterns are full-size and ready to duplicate immediately. Patterns for larger projects are shown on a grid that can be scaled up to size, easily and accurately.

Many people have made this book possible. They are the artists, craftspeople, designers and teachers who have discovered the joy in working with their hands and to whom adding their own loving touches to Christmas is important. Their names accompany each project. May you have as much fun with these ideas as we have. Enjoy the season and have the most glorious Christmas ever!

— *Anna Hobbs*

CHAPTER 1

Christmas All Through the House

A Country Christmas

Savor the simple joys of an old-fashioned Christmas with fun and folksy decorating ideas.
There's a charming wooden village to adorn a mantel or tabletop, perky papier-mâché birds and
wonderful wooden reindeer. Each decoration is guaranteed to be an absorbing project for the entire
family. Complete the country theme with table linens and accessories and a Starry Night Stocking.

Wooden Village

Design by Jane Buckles

YOU NEED

- Softwood (such as knot-free pine), one piece 2 x 6 in. x 8 ft. (5.0 x 15.0 cm x 2.44 m), for buildings*, and one piece 1 x 8 x 34 in. (2.5 x 20.0 x 86.4 cm), for trees and mill wheel

- 3/8 x 3/4 in. (1.0 x 2.0 cm) balsa wood strip, 30 in. (76 cm) long

- Scraps of 1/4 in. (0.6 cm) dowelling, for lightning rod and barber pole

- 2 1/2 in. (6.0 cm) and 1 1/4 in. (3.2 cm) spiral nails

- White craft glue

- Sandpaper

- X-ACTO knife

- Saw and jigsaw

- Hammer

- Vise

- Gesso or wood primer

- Acrylic paint in assorted colors

- Artist's paintbrushes

- Pencil with new eraser on end

- Spray varnish

- Letraset transferable lettering

*At a lumberyard or where an electric table saw is available, cut this piece into 33 in. (83.8 cm) and 63 in. (160 cm) lengths. On 33 in. length, cut off one long edge at a 60° angle as shown in Diagram 1. On 63 in. length, cut off one long edge at a 45° angle as shown in Diagram 2.

Note: Sand all edges of wooden blocks as they are cut. Refer to diagrams as you proceed.

Barn   C   Mill   B   D

HOUSES A AND F, SHOPS B AND C

From angled 33 in. (83.8 cm) length of pine, cut off:

- two 5 1/2 in. (14.0 cm) lengths, for house A
- two 4 in. (10.0 cm) lengths, for house F
- four 3 1/2 in. (9.0 cm) lengths, for shops B and C

Glue and nail pieces of same size together in pairs in shape of basic building shown in Diagram 3.

SHOP D, HOUSE E, CHURCH, BARN AND MILL

From angled 63 in. (160.0 cm) length of pine, cut off:

- one 6 1/2 in. (16.5 cm) length, for shop D
- one 25 in. (63.5 cm) length, for house E and church
- two 5 3/4 in. (14.6 cm) lengths, for barn
- three 4 1/2 in. (11.0 cm) lengths, for mill
- one 3 1/2 in. (9.0 cm) length, for mill

1. **Shop D:** Cut 1 1/4 in. (3.2 cm) off long unangled bottom edge of 6 1/2 in. (16.5 cm) length (see Diagram 4). Set scrap aside for church. Cut piece in half vertically so you have two 3 1/4 in. (8.3 cm) lengths. Glue and nail these two pieces together in shape of basic building shown in Diagram 3.

2. **House E:** Cut 3/4 in. (2.0 cm) off long unangled bottom edge of 25 in. (63.5 cm) length (see Diagram 5). Discard scrap. Cut piece vertically into five 5 in. (12.5 cm) lengths. Set aside two of these pieces for church. Glue and nail two pieces together in shape of basic building shown in Diagram 3. Cut 1 1/4 in. (3.2 cm) off unangled bottom edge of remaining piece, and then cut in half vertically, as shown in Diagram 6. Discard shaded parts. Glue and nail remaining part onto side of house to form porch (Diagram 7).

3. **Church:** Glue and nail together two 5 in. (12.5 cm) pieces set aside in Step 2 in shape of basic building shown in Diagram 3. From scrap saved from shop D, cut a 4 1/2 in. (11.0 cm) length, to make a block 1 1/4 x 1 3/4 x 4 1/2 in. (3.2 x 4.5 x 11.0 cm). Measure and mark cutting lines on block, as shown in Diagram 8. Cut along dotted lines to form church steeple. Glue steeple in place on top of one end of church (Diagram 9).

4. **Barn:** Glue and nail two 5 3/4 in. (14.6 cm) lengths together in shape of basic building shown in Diagram 3. From scrap, cut a 1 x 1 1/4 x 2 in. (2.5 x 3.2 x 5.0 cm) block for cupola. Measure and mark cutting lines on block, as shown in Diagram 10. Cut along dotted lines. Glue cupola in place on center of barn roof. Drill a 1/4 in. (6.35 mm) diameter hole in center top of cupola. Glue and insert a 1 3/4 in. (4.5 cm) length of dowelling (threaded with bead, if desired) in hole to form lightning rod (Diagram 11).

5. **Mill:** Glue and nail two 4 1/2 in. (11.0 cm) lengths together in shape of basic building shown in Diagram 3. For shed, cut 2 in. (5.0 cm) off unangled bottom edge of remaining 4 1/2 in. length. Glue and nail onto side of mill (Diagram 12). For front porch, cut 1 1/2 in. (4.0 cm) off unangled bottom edge of 3 1/2 in. (9.0 cm) length, and then cut in half vertically, as shown in Diagram 13. Discard shaded parts. Glue and nail remaining part onto front end of mill to form porch (Diagram 12). Mill wheel will be cut later.

TREES AND MILL WHEEL

Enlarge patterns for trees and mill wheel by the squaring method (see General Directions, page 130) directly onto 1 x 8 x 34 in. (2.5 x 20.0 x 86.4 cm) pine, instead of using brown paper. Cut out pieces with saw and jigsaw. Glue mill wheel onto side of mill (Diagram 12).

TO FINISH:

Sand all pieces thoroughly.

33"
60°
6"
2"
Diagram 1

63"
45°
6"
2"
Diagram 2

Diagram 3
Basic building

3-1/4"
1-1/4"
Diagram 4
Shop D

5"   5"   5"   5"   5"
3/4"
Diagram 5   House E

1-1/4"
Diagram 6

porch
Diagram 7
House E

repeat peak
line of church
roof
trace peak
line of
church
4-1/2"
1-3/4" 1-1/4"
Diagram 8
Church steeple

repeat peak
line of barn roof
trace peak
line of barn roof
2"
1-1/4" 1"
Diagram 10
Barn cupola

Diagram 9
Church

Diagram 11
Barn

shed
porch
wheel
Diagram 12
Mill

1-1/2"
Diagram 13
Porch

3/4"
1"
Diagram 14
Chimney

Diagram 15
Eraser stamp

mill wheel
deciduous trees
pine trees
Trees and Mill Wheel

1. **House A:** With small handsaw, cut two 5 3/4 in. (14.6 cm) lengths of balsa wood. Glue one strip to each end of house for chimneys.

2. **Shops B and C:** Cut four 1 in. (2.5 cm) lengths of balsa wood for chimneys. Cut bottom edge of each chimney at an angle to correspond to angle of roof (Diagram 14). Glue chimneys in place.

3. **Houses E and F:** Cut two 5 1/2 in. (14.0 cm) lengths from the balsa wood. Glue one strip to the end of each house for the chimneys.

TO PAINT:
Paint your village as desired. Ours has been painted to depict the summer season on one side of each building and the Christmas season on the other. Trees show summer leaves on one side and bare winter branches on the other. Refer to photo for suggested colors and designs.

Here are a few painting tips:

1. Paint all parts with gesso or similar primer paint.

2. Work from large to small, allowing paint to dry before applying next color. First paint the walls and roof; then window and door shapes; then shutters, door frames and trim lines; and finally, the small decorative details such as flowers in window boxes, wreaths, baked goods in bakery window, barber pole, snow, etc.

3. **Window panes:** With X-ACTO knife, cut eraser on end of pencil into a rectangle (Diagram 15). Use this to stamp panes on windows and around doors.

4. **Signs:** Letraset sign names on paper, then cut out and glue onto buildings with white craft glue. Paint glue over sign to seal.

5. Allow paint to dry thoroughly. Spray-varnish all buildings.

Twig Reindeer

Design by Jane Buckles

*Larger reindeer on wheels stands 9 in. (23.0 cm) high.
Smaller reindeer suitable for tree decoration measures
7 in. (18.0 cm) high.*

YOU NEED

FOR LARGER REINDEER:

- Logs with or without bark, preferably softwood such as pine or cedar, in the following dimensions:

  1 1/2 in. (4.0 cm) diameter, cut into one piece 2 1/2 in. (6.0 cm) long, for head, and four pieces 1/2 in. (1.3 cm) long, for wheels

  2 1/2 in. (6.0 cm) diameter, 5 to 6 in. (12.5 to 15.0 cm) long, for body

- Dowelling in the following dimensions:

  four pieces, 1/2 in. (1.3 cm) diameter, each 5 3/4 in. (14.6 cm) long, for legs

  one piece, 3/4 in. (2.0 cm) diameter, 1 1/2 in. (4.0 cm) long, for neck

  two pieces, 1/4 in. (0.6 cm) diameter, each 1 1/4 in. (3.2 cm) long, for ears, OR two 1/4 in. (0.6 cm) dowel pins (available at lumber or hardware stores)

  five pieces, 3/8 in. (1.0 cm) diameter, each 1 1/4 in. (3.2 cm) long, for tail and axles, OR five 3/8 in. (1.0 cm) dowel pins

  four pieces, 1/8 in. (0.3 cm) diameter, each 1 in. (2.5 cm) long, for axle pins

- Scrap of pine, 1 x 3 x 4 1/2 in. (2.5 x 7.5 x 11.0 cm), for base

- Two antler-shaped branches (apple tree branches and twigs work well)

- Two wooden hole plugs, 3/8 in. (1.0 cm) diameter, for eyes (available at most lumber and hardware stores)

FOR SMALLER REINDEER:

- Logs, as described above, in the following dimensions:

  1 3/4 in. (4.5 cm) diameter, 3 in. (7.5 cm) long, for body

  1 1/4 in. (3.2 cm) diameter, 1 3/4 in. (4.5 cm) long, for head

- Dowelling in the following dimensions:

  four pieces, 3/8 in. (1.0 cm) diameter, each 3 in. (7.5 cm) long, for legs

  one piece, 3/8 in. (1.0 cm) diameter, 1 1/2 in. (4.0 cm) long, for neck

  three 1/4 in. (0.6 cm) dowel pins, for ears and tail

- Two small wooden hole plugs, 1/4 in. (0.6 cm) diameter, for eyes

- Two small antler-shaped branches, for antlers

- One small screw eye

FOR BOTH PROJECTS:

- Electric drill with assortment of bits to correspond to diameter of dowelling and branches

- Saw

- Glue gun and glue sticks or white craft glue

Note: *Refer to diagrams as you proceed.*

1. In one end of head and one end of body, drill holes 3/4 in. (2.0 cm) deep for large reindeer, or 1/2 in. (1.3 cm) deep for smaller reindeer. Glue and insert neck dowelling into holes to join head to body.

2. Drill two holes for ears on either side of head, two holes for eyes in top of head and one hole for tail in tail end. Glue and insert appropriate dowel pins.

3. Drill four holes for legs in bottom of body. Glue and insert legs.

4. Drill two holes for antler branches on top of head behind eyes. Glue and insert antler branches.

5. Tie decorative ribbon or bell around neck or antlers, if desired. For smaller reindeer tree decoration, insert screw eye into top of body close to head and then attach a hanging thread.

For larger reindeer only, proceed as follows:

6. Stand reindeer on base and mark positions for four leg holes. Drill holes 1/4 in. (0.6 cm) deep. With 3/8 in. (9.525 mm) drill bit, clamping wood in vise if necessary, carefully drill two holes in each side of base under each leg.

7. With 1/2 in. (12.7 mm) drill bit, drill a hole all the way through center of each log wheel. With 1/8 in. (3.175 mm) drill bit, drill hole near one end of each axle, all the way through.

8. To assemble, insert 1/8 in. (0.3 cm) axle pins through hole in end of each axle. Insert axles through wheels and then glue into holes on sides of base. Glue and insert legs into holes in top of base.

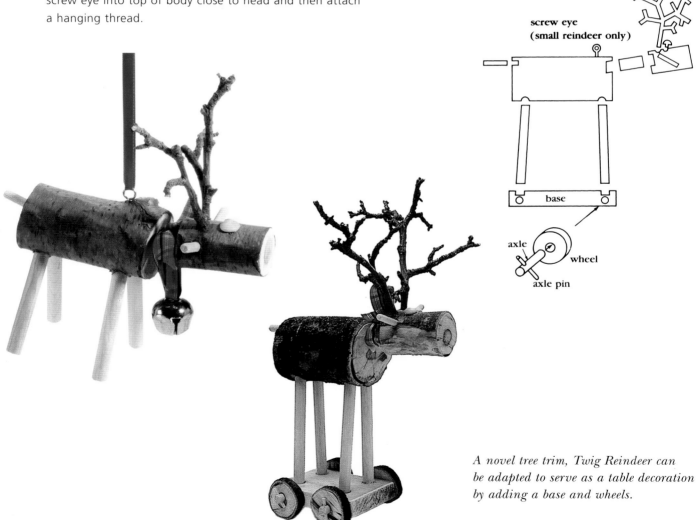

TWIG REINDEER

screw eye
(small reindeer only)

base

axle   wheel

axle pin

A novel tree trim, Twig Reindeer can be adapted to serve as a table decoration by adding a base and wheels.

Brown Bag Buildings

Design by Jo Calvert

> ### YOU NEED
>
> - Plain brown bags with flat bottoms
> - Black construction paper
> - Felt-tip markers in assorted colors
> - Scraps of ribbon
> - Scraps of lightweight cardboard (optional)
> - Scissors
> - Ruler
> - Hole punch

1. With markers, draw simple shapes for door, windows, shutters, etc., on front and back of flat bag, referring to photo (below), if desired. Open bag and place upright. If desired, stiffen bottom of bag by measuring bottom and then cutting and fitting a piece of cardboard inside.

2. Place gift in bag. Fold down top of bag. For roof, cut a piece of black paper the width of front of bag. Fold paper in half, parallel to width, and place over top of bag. Trim away excess paper so roof is desired height. Punch holes through all layers approx. 3/4 in. (2.0 cm) below fold. Thread ribbons through holes and tie to close.

Fabric Sacks

Design by Jo Calvert

> ### YOU NEED
>
> - Scraps of printed or plain cotton fabric
> - Scraps of ribbon
> - Ruler
> - Matching thread

1. From fabric, cut a pair of rectangular, square or stocking shapes slightly larger than desired finished size. Press under 1/4 in. (0.6 cm), then 1/4 in. again, along one edge (top edge) of each piece. Stitch.

2. From contrasting colored fabric, cut two casing strips. Each strip should be 3/4 in. (approx. 2.0 cm) shorter than width of top edge and 1 1/8 in. (approx 3.0 cm) wider than ribbon. Press under 3/8 in. (1.0 cm) along all casing strip edges. On right side, center each strip parallel to and approx. 1 5/8 in. (4.0 cm) from top edges. Edgestitch in place along long edges.

3. If desired, machine-appliqué initial or name to one fabric piece. With right sides together, stitch, using a 3/8 in. (1.0 cm) seam allowance and leaving top edge open. Clip corners or curves. Bind raw edges of seam allowance with zigzag stitching, if desired. Turn sack right-side out.

4. Thread ribbon through each casing. Pull up tightly and tie a bow at each side of bag.

Bird on a Swing

Design by Jane Buckles

YOU NEED

- Styrofoam egg, 4 x 3 in. (10.0 x 7.5 cm)
- Coat hanger wire, one 14 in. (35.5 cm) length and four 3 1/2 in. (9.0 cm) lengths
- 1/2 in. (1.3 cm) dowelling, one piece 4 1/2 in. (11.0 cm) long and one piece 1 in. (2.5 cm) long
- Two wooden beads, approx. 3/8 in. (0.8 cm) in diameter, for eyes
- One small feather
- 1/4 yd. (0.20 m) factory cotton (unbleached muslin)
- Newspaper
- Wallpaper paste
- Glue gun and glue sticks (optional)
- White craft glue
- Gesso
- Acrylic paint in assorted colors
- Artist's paintbrushes
- Spray varnish
- Saw
- Pliers
- Wire cutter
- Scissors
- File or sandpaper
- Electric drill with bit to correspond to diameter of wire

1. **Perch:** Bend 14 in. (35.5 cm) length of wire in half, then, using pliers, shape each half into perch as shown in Diagram 1. Drill a hole 1/4 in. (0.6 cm) from each end of 4 1/2 in. (11.0 cm) length of dowelling to fit wire. Insert and glue ends of wire in holes (see Diagram 2). With small end up, position Styrofoam egg on perch, and with a knife, carve a narrow groove in the underside of egg to accommodate perch. Egg will be glued to perch along this groove later.

2. **Beak:** Sand or file one end of 1 in. (2.5 cm) length of dowelling into a dull point. Push opposite end into head at beak level and glue in place.

3. **Body:** Mix up approx. 1 cup (250 mL) wallpaper paste to ketchup-like consistency. Add about 1/4 cup (50 mL) white craft glue. Tear newspaper into approx. 1 1/2 x 1 in. (4.0 x 2.5 cm) pieces. Smear egg with lots of paste and glue on one layer of newspaper pieces, overlapping pieces generously as you go, leaving beak uncovered and retaining groove for perch. Set aside to dry thoroughly. Glue bird to perch.

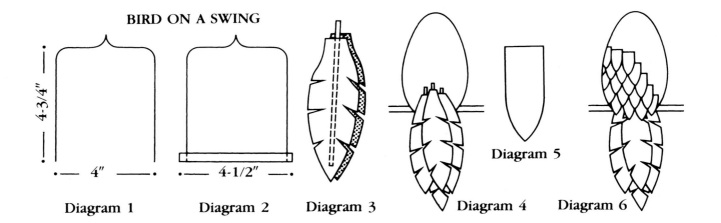

BIRD ON A SWING

4-3/4"

4"

Diagram 1

4-1/2"

Diagram 2

Diagram 3

Diagram 4

Diagram 5

Diagram 6

4. **Tail feathers:** From muslin, cut eight tail feathers approx. 3 x 1 in. (7.5 x 2.5 cm), as shown in Diagram 3. Clip sides as shown. Soak all feathers in paste. Glue feathers together in pairs, sandwiching a 3 1/2 in. (9.0 cm) length of wire between each pair (end of wire should extend beyond base of feathers). Push each tail feather into tail end of bird, as shown in Diagram 4.

5. **Feathers:** From muslin, cut fifty to sixty small feathers, approx. 1 1/2 x 5/8 in. (4.0 x 1.5 cm), and tiny feathers, approx. 1/4 x 1 in. (0.6 x 2.5 cm), as shown in Diagram 5. Soak all feathers in paste. Starting at tail end of bird, glue small feathers to body in overlapping rows around base of tail and entire body up to head (Diagram 6). Glue tiny feathers to head in overlapping rows radiating out from beak. Hang to dry.

6. Glue on eyes. Paint perch desired color. Let dry.

7. Paint bird with gesso. Let dry. Paint bird in desired colors. Refer to photo for suggested colors and designs. Paint beak and eyes. When dry, spray-varnish.

8. Poke a small hole in top of head. Insert feather and glue in place.

Starry Night Stocking

Design by Jo Calvert

YOU NEED

- 5/8 yd. (0.50 m) red calico, 45 in. (approx. 115.0 cm) wide, for lining, binding and ties
- 5/8 yd. (0.50 m) unbleached muslin, 45 in. (115.0 cm) wide, for interlining
- Piece of blue calico, 20.0 x 12.0 in. (approx. 50.0 x 30.0 cm), for sky
- Scraps of solid and printed cotton in assorted colors, white and natural, for appliqué
- Two pieces of polyester batting, each 20 x 16 in. (approx. 50.0 x 40.0 cm)
- Small gold sequin stars
- Matching thread
- Dressmaker's chalk pencil
- Brown paper

To enlarge pattern, see General Directions (page 130).

Note: A 3/8 in. (1.0 cm) seam allowance is included along *outside edges of stocking only*. Solid lines indicate cutting lines for paper pattern. Dotted lines indicate decorative stitching lines.

1. From brown paper, cut out patterns for main stocking shapes along outer edges (bold lines) only. From batting, muslin and red calico, cut stocking front and back. From red calico, cut three strips 20.0 x 2 1/8 in. (approx. 50.0 x 5.5 cm). Set aside.

2. Cut paper pattern along inner (thin) solid lines. Lay all pattern pieces on right side of appropriate colored fabric (see color labels on pattern). With dressmaker's chalk pencil, trace around each pattern piece, leaving at least 5/8 in. (1.5 cm) between pieces on same fabric.

3. Cut fabric as follows: Along underlap edges (indicated by small arrows), cut 1/4 in. (0.6 cm) out from traced lines for underlap allowance. Along remaining overlap and outside edges, cut along traced lines.

4. Assemble stocking front and back, matching cut edges of overlaps with chalk lines on underlaps. Baste. With wrong sides together, baste one muslin stocking to stocking front and the other to stocking back, along outside edges. Using matching thread and a wide, closely spaced zigzag stitch, appliqué pieces together. Stitch decorative stitching lines as indicated. To finish each stitching line neatly, pull threads to wrong side. Knot close to fabric and clip.

5. Sandwich one batting stocking between wrong sides of stocking front and lining. Baste together around outside edges. Using white thread and straight stitch, machine-quilt around outline of appliqué shapes and along horizontal lines in sky indicated by broken lines. Repeat for stocking back.

6. With right sides together and using a 3/8 in. (1.0 cm) seam allowance, stitch stocking front to back, leaving top edge open. Clip curves. Trim seam allowance to 1/4 in. (0.6 cm). Bind raw edges of seam allowance to 1/4 in. Bind raw edges of seam allowance with zigzag stitch. Remove basting.

7. For stocking ties, press under 3/8 in. (1.0 cm) along

two long edges and one short end of two red calico strips. Fold each in half so folded edges meet. Topstitch folded edges together. With raw ends of ties and top edge of stocking even, baste ties, one on top of another, at back seam.

8. For binding, press under 3/8 in. (1.0 cm) along one long edge and one short end of remaining red calico strip. With right side of strip and wrong side of stocking together, pin unfolded long edge around top edge of

stocking. Lap short raw end over folded end approx. 1/4 in. (0.6 cm) and trim away excess binding. Stitch. Turn stocking right-side out. Fold and pin binding over and down 5/8 in. (1.5 cm) from top edge of stocking. Edgestitch top and bottom of binding through all layers, catching tie ends in stitching. Fold ties upward and zigzag across bottom edge. Tie ends of ties into a bow.

9. Hand-stitch star sequins to sky as desired.

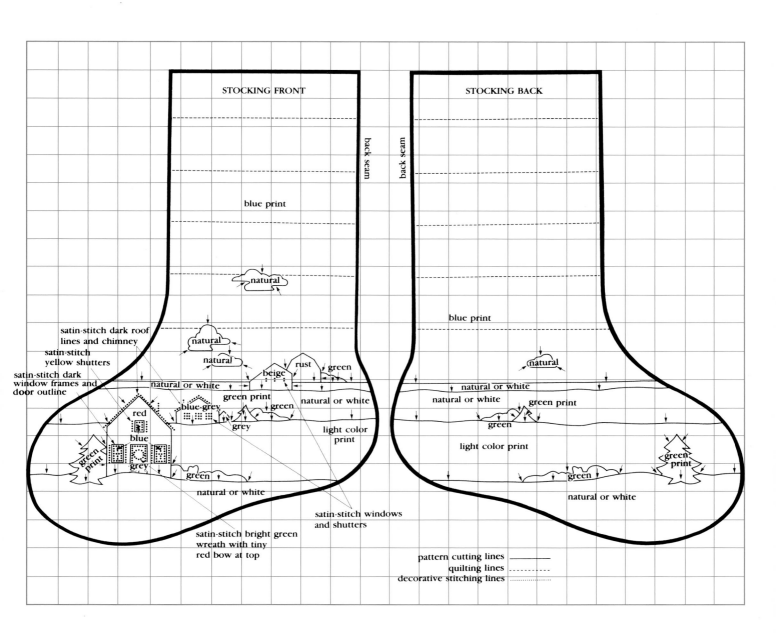

Woodland Songbird

Design by Carol Moore

A few twigs and berries, a little bird in its nest and a bright bow. It couldn't be simpler. Add country charm to a mantel, a table or a shelf any time of the year, but especially at Christmas, when it will also make an original tree decoration.

YOU NEED

- **Twenty grapevine twigs approx. 6 in. (15.0 cm) long**
- **Two or three twigs of curly willow approx. 6 in. (15.0 cm) long**
- **Heavy twine**
- **Two sprigs of artificial berries**
- **Craft moss**
- **One small artificial bird**
- **1 1/3 yd. (1.20 m) wire-edged ribbon, 1 3/8 in. (3.5 cm) wide**
- **Glue gun**

1. Gather grapevine and willow twigs together in a bundle and wrap twine three or four times around center. Knot securely.

2. Shape moss into a little nest, rolling the fibers slightly so the ends don't stick out. Glue nest to twig bundle, covering the knotted twine. Glue bird in nest.

3. Make a four-loop bow and glue it in place just beneath the nest. Glue sprigs of berries to twigs.

Reindeer Wall Plaque

Design by Jane Buckles

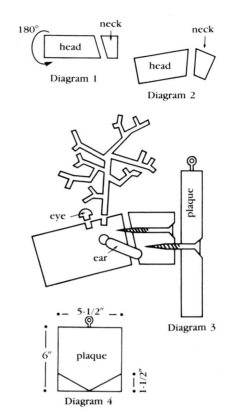

Diagram 1

Diagram 2

Diagram 3

Diagram 4

YOU NEED

- **One log, as described for twig reindeer (page 13), 2 1/2 in. (6.0 cm) diameter, 5 in. (12.5) long, for head/neck**
- **Two 3/8 in. (1.0 cm) dowel pins, for ears**
- **Two wooden hole plugs, 3/8 in. (1.0 cm) diameter, for eyes (available at most lumber and hardware stores)**
- **Scrap of pine, 1 x 5 1/2 x 6 in. (2.5 x 14.0 x 15.0 cm), for plaque**
- **Two antler-shaped branches**
- **One small screw eye**
- **Two screws, 2 1/2 in. (6.0 cm) long**
- **Electric drill with 3/8 in. (9.525 mm) bit, inset bit and bit to correspond to size of screws**
- **Saw**
- **Glue gun and glue sticks or white craft glue**

Note: Refer to diagrams as you proceed.

1. Cut log at a very slight angle, as shown in Diagram 1. Turn longer end of log (head) around 180° so it is at an angle to the shorter piece (neck), as shown in Diagram 2.

2. With neck and head pieces held together, drill hole through neck into head using a drill bit same size as screw (see Diagram 3). Glue and screw neck to head. Insert screw so it does not stick out at back of neck.

3. Cut angles at one end of plaque as shown in Diagram 4. Insert screw eye into center of top edge.

4. Position head/neck on plaque slightly below center. Drill hole through back of plaque into neck. Glue and screw plaque to head/neck. Inset screw.

5. Drill two holes for ears in side of head, two holes for eyes in top of head and two holes for antler branches behind eyes. Glue all parts in place.

6. Tie decorative ribbon or bell around neck or antlers, if desired.

Simple Strip Patchwork

Design by Jo Calvert

YOU NEED

- Short lengths or scraps of printed or plain cottons
- Matching thread
- Dressmaker's chalk pencil
- Yardstick or meter-stick

To make patchwork pieces:

Patchwork is made up of fabric strips of various widths cut on straight grain and sewn together into one piece. Length and number of strips necessary are determined by size of patchwork piece needed for each project. Refer to specific instructions for required sizes.

1. Press all fabric. Using yardstick and chalk pencil, measure, mark and accurately cut strips of desired width and length on crosswise or lengthwise straight grain of fabric. Remember to include extra width for seam allowances.

2. Select a center strip. You may wish to choose a color that matches backing/border fabric. Arrange remaining strips as desired on either side of center strip so that design is symmetrical.

3. With right sides together and using a closely spaced machine stitch, sew one long edge of center strip and one long edge of adjoining right-hand strip together. Sew other long edge of center strip to adjoining left-hand strip in same manner. Continue sewing adjoining strips together, alternating from right- to left-hand side to prevent curling.

Table Runner

Design by Jo Calvert

Finished runner measures 70 x 12 1/2 in. (178.0 x 32.0 cm). You may wish to adjust length for size of your table.

YOU NEED

- Piece of patchwork, 12 1/2 in. (32.0 cm) square
- Two pieces of patchwork (having strips parallel to long edges), each 29 1/2 x 12 1/2 in. (75.0 x 32.0 cm)
- Piece of plain or printed cotton, 74 x 16 1/4 in. (187.0 x 41.0 cm), for backing
- Piece of polyester batting, 70 1/4 x 12 1/2 (178.0 x 32.0 cm)
- Thread to match backing
- Dressmaker's chalk pencil
- Ruler

1. With right sides together, stitch patchwork square to one short end of one patchwork rectangle, so that strips run at right angles to each other. With right sides together, stitch one short end of remaining patchwork rectangle to opposite edge of square. Press seams open.

2. Read Note and follow Steps 1 and 2 of place mat instructions (page 23).

3. Pin patchwork to backing every 2 in. (approx. 5.0 cm) along edges of strips, with pins at right angles to long edges to prevent fabric from shifting as you quilt. Machine-quilt center patchwork square as for place mat, working from center strip outward. Machine-quilt patchwork rectangles from edge of square to chalk line in same manner.

4. Make borders as for place mat, Step 4.

Place Mat and Napkin

Design by Jo Calvert

YOU NEED

For one place mat and napkin:

- Piece of patchwork (having strips parallel to long edges), 17 x 12 in. (45.0 x 32.0 cm)

- Piece of printed or plain cotton, 20 1/2 x 15 1/2 in. (54.0 x 41.0 cm), for backing

- Piece of printed or plain cotton, 15 in. (40.0 cm) square, for napkin

- Piece of polyester batting, 17 x 12 in. (45.0 x 32.0 cm)

- Thread to match backing

- Dressmaker's chalk pencil

- Ruler

Note: For a neat finish to quilting lines, pull thread ends through to back of work. Knot ends close to fabric, two at a time, then thread back between fabric layers for approx. 3/4 in. (2.0 cm) and out again. Clip.

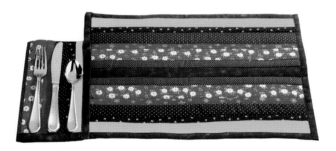

Finished place mat measures 17 x 12 in. (45.0 x 32.0 cm).

1. On right side of patchwork, measure and mark a chalk line 5/8 in. (1.5 cm) in from each raw edge.

2. Lay backing wrong-side up on a flat working surface; center batting on top and then center patchwork, right-side up, on top of batting. Baste around edges through all layers.

3. Pin patchwork to backing every 2 in. (approx. 5.0 cm) along edges of strips, with pins at right angles to long edges to prevent fabric from shifting as you quilt.

Working from center strip outward, machine-quilt by edge stitching long edges of each strip from chalk line to chalk line.

4. Lay mat down, backing-side up. Press under 5/8 in. (1.5 cm) along all edges. Turn mat over, patchwork-side up. To form border, wrap backing around each short edge of mat so folded edge meets chalk line. Pin. Wrap backing around long edges in same manner so long borders overlap short borders neatly at corners. Pin. Slipstitch overlaps at corners. Edgestitch inner and outer edges of border around mat. Remove basting.

5. To make napkin, turn under 1/4 in. (0.6 cm), then 1/4 in. again around all edges. Stitch.

Hot Mat

Design by Jo Calvert

Finished hot mat measures 12 1/2 in. (32.0 cm) square.

YOU NEED

- Piece of patchwork 12 1/2 in. (32.0 cm) square

- Piece of printed or plain cotton, 16 in. (41.0 cm) square, for backing

- Piece of thermal interlining (compressed batting with

  shiny foil on one side), 12 1/2 in. (32.0 cm) square

- Thread to match backing

- Dressmaker's chalk pencil

- Ruler

Follow Steps 1 to 4 of place mat instructions (this page), being sure to have shiny side of thermal batting facing up in Step 2.

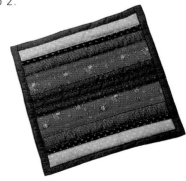

Pot Holder

Design by Jo Calvert

Finished pot holder measures 9 in. (approx. 23.0 cm) square.

YOU NEED

- Piece of patchwork, 9 in. (approx. 23.0 cm) square
- Piece of printed or plain cotton, 9 in. (23.0 cm) square, for backing
- Piece of thermal interlining (compressed batting with shiny foil on one side), 9 in. (23.0 cm) square
- 1 1/4 yd. (1.10 m) printed or plain wide double-fold bias tape
- Thread to match backing
- Ruler

1. Follow Steps 1 to 3 of place mat instructions, being sure to have shiny side of thermal batting facing down in Step 2. When quilting is complete, slightly round all corners with scissors.

2. Cut a 5 1/2 in. (14.0 cm) length of bias tape. Stitch long folded edges together. To make a loop, fold in half so short ends meet. Pin loop to right side of pot holder at one corner, having raw edges of loop and pot holder even. Cut a 37 1/2 in. (approx. 95.0 cm) length of bias tape. Pin around pot holder, enclosing raw edges in fold. Stitch. Fold loop away from pot holder, and zigzag across bottom edge. Remove basting.

Bun Basket Napkin

Design by Jo Calvert

Finished napkin is 21 in. (53.0 cm) square.

YOU NEED

- Four patched triangles, each with one long edge of 8 3/4 in. (approx. 22.5 cm) having patched strips parallel to long edge, and two short edges of 6 1/4 in. (approx. 16.0 cm), having a right angle at their junction (see Diagram at right)
- Two pieces of printed or plain cotton, each 21 5/8 in. (approx. 55.0 cm) square
- Thread to match cotton squares
- Dressmaker's chalk pencil
- Ruler

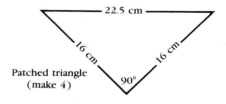

Patched triangle
(make 4)

— 22.5 cm —
16 cm   16 cm
90°

1. Lay one cotton square, right-side up, on a flat working surface. From each corner, measure 5 1/8 in. (13.0 cm) along edge in each direction and mark with chalk pencil. Draw a straight line across each corner from one marked point to the other. Cut off corners along drawn lines. With right sides together and long edge of each triangle even with and centered over each cut edge at corners, stitch four triangles in place using a 3/8 in. (1.0 cm) seam allowance. Press seams open.

2. With right sides together, stitch patched square to remaining cotton square, using a 3/8 in. (1.0 cm) seam allowance and leaving open along one edge. Clip corners. Turn right-side out. Press under 3/8 in. (1.0 cm) around opening. Pin together. Press other edges flat. Edgestitch all edges of napkin. Machine-quilt corners by edgestitching strips.

Patchwork Apron

Design by Jo Calvert

YOU NEED

- **Piece of patchwork (having strips parallel to long edges), 32 x 9 1/2 in. (approx. 82.0 x 24.0 cm)**
- **1 1/2 yd. (1.30 m) printed or plain cotton, 45 (approx. 115.0 cm) wide**
- **Matching thread**
- **Ruler**
- **Brown paper**

1. From cotton, cut apron, one strip 21 1/2 x 2 3/4 in. (55.0 x 7.0 cm), two strips each 31 1/2 x 2 3/4 in. (80.0 x 7.0 cm) and one rectangle 32 x 9 1/2 in. (82.0 x 24.0 cm).

2. Clip curved side edges of apron, turn under 1/4 in. (0.6 cm), and then 1/4 in. again. Topstitch. Hem remaining side, top and bottom edges, in same manner.

3. **Neck loop:** Press under 3/8 in. (1.0 cm) along both long edges of short strip. Fold in half so folded edges meet. Pin. Edgestitch all edges. Press under 1/4 in. (0.6 cm) at both ends. Pin ends to top corners of apron indicated by Xs. Topstitch in place along dotted lines.

4. **Waist ties:** Press under 3/8 in. (1.0 cm) along both long edges and one short end of each long strip. Fold in half so folded edges meet. Pin. Edgestitch all edges. Press under 1/4 in. (0.6 cm) at remaining raw end, and then pin to apron at each side corner indicated by Xs. Topstitch ties in place along dotted lines.

5. **Pocket:** With right sides together and using a 3/8 in. (1.0 cm) seam allowance, stitch patchwork rectangle to cotton rectangle, leaving open along one short edge. Clip corners. Turn right-side out. Press under 3/8 in. around opening. Slipstitch opening closed. Press. Edgestitch one long edge (top edge).

6. Pin and machine-quilt patchwork pocket as for place mat, Step 3.

7. Lay quilted patchwork pocket, right-side up, on front of apron so bottom and side edges are even. Pin. Edgestitch pocket to apron along bottom and side edges. Divide pocket into four equal segments with vertical rows of stitching.

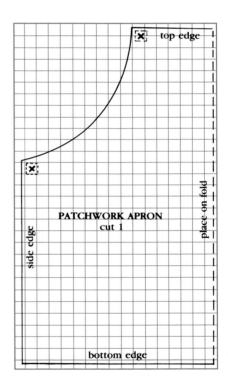

Heavenly Choir

DESIGN BY CAROL MOORE

Bring the spirit of Christmas into your home with a chorus of angelic choir girls. Each caroler is simple to construct using a cardboard cone, a Styrofoam ball and bits of fabric — no sewing required.

YOU NEED

Quantities are given for Small size choir girl. Any changes for Medium and Large sizes are written in brackets. If there is only one set of figures, it applies to all three sizes.

- Styrofoam ball, 1 1/2 [2, 2] in. (approx. 4.0 [5.0, 5.0] cm) in diameter
- 4 in. (approx. 10.0 cm) square of Dip 'N Drape fabric or cotton muslin and fabric stiffener, available at craft supply stores
- White 8-ply poster board, 8 1/4 x 6 1/4 [9 1/2 x 6 3/4, 12 5/8 x 9 1/2] in. (approx. 21.0 x 16.0 [24.0 x 17.0, 32.0 x 24.0] cm), for body
- White sheer drapery fabric as follows: 9 x 6 3/4 [11 x 7 5/8, 12 1/4 x 10 1/4] in. (approx. 23.0 x 17.0 [27.5 x 19.5, 31.0 x 26.0] cm), for dress, and 7 x 3 [10 x 3 1/2, 11 x 4] in.

- (18.0 x 7.5 [25.0 x 9.0, 27.5 x 10.0] cm), for sleeves
- 6 3/4 [8, 9] in. (17.0 [20.0, 23.0] cm) of 24-gauge wire, for arms
- Natural sheep's fleece, for hair
- Straight pin
- White facial tissue
- Wooden skewer or knitting needle
- 5/8 yd. (0.50 m) satin ribbon, approx. 3/16 in. (0.5 cm) wide
- Birthday candle or white paper
- Gesso (white under coat and sealer)
- Black, red and flesh-tone acrylic paint
- Artist's paintbrush
- Glue gun and glue sticks or white craft glue
- Elastic bands
- Brown paper

Small choir girl stands 6 3/4 in. (17.0 cm) tall. Medium stands 7 7/8 in. (20.0 cm) tall and large 9 1/2 in. (24.0 cm) tall.

To enlarge pattern, see General Directions (page 130).

1. Roll half of Styrofoam ball along a sharp counter or table edge, making an indentation from one side of ball to other, for face (see Diagram for side view). Cut out a 3/8 in. (1.0 cm) piece of Styrofoam from back of head, for nose. Press it between fingers to make a small ball about the size of a pea. With straight pin, attach nose to center of face along indentation line. Place Dip 'N Drape fabric into very warm water for 5 seconds and then shake off excess water or soak muslin in fabric stiffener. Center square over nose and mold it with fingers to fit around nose, cheeks, hairline and chin area. Set aside to dry in a warm place for about 4 hours. When face is dry and hard, paint with two coats of gesso, allowing to dry at least 3 hours after each coat. Paint face with flesh-colored paint. Let dry. With point of skewer or knitting needle, poke a hole just below the nose, and with a circular motion make an oval or circular hole for mouth. Paint eyes and inside of mouth with black paint. Put a tiny drop of red paint on your finger and gently rub into cheeks.

2. **Body:** Trace body pattern onto poster board. Cut out. Roll up sides to form a cone. Glue and hold together until dry. Apply glue to top of cone and push partway into head.

3. **Dress:** Fold dress fabric in half so short edges meet and right sides are together. Glue short edges together. Carefully turn right-side out and slip tube over figure so seam is at back. Apply glue around neck. Pleat and gather fabric around neck, making a 3/4 to 1 in. (2.0 to 2.5 cm) ruffle under chin. Hold gathers in place with elastic band until glue dries. Tuck and glue fabric at bottom of dress to inside of cone. Tie a small bow in middle of a 13 3/4 in. (approx. 35.0 cm) length of ribbon and then glue to front of dress just under ruffle at chin.

4. **Arms:** Fold sleeve fabric in half so long edges meet and wrong sides are together. Glue long edges together. Twist and glue a piece of tissue around wire so it is completely covered. Poke wire through sleeve tube.

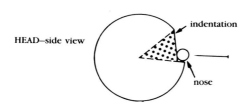

HEAD—side view

indentation

nose

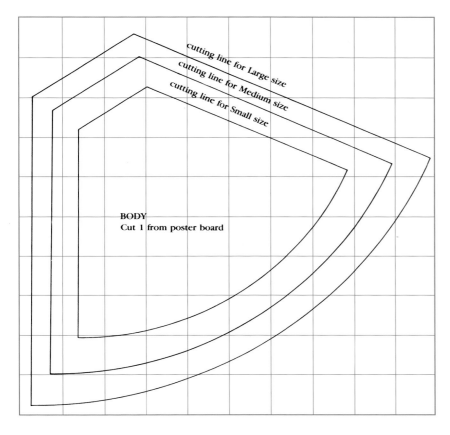

cutting line for Large size

cutting line for Medium size

cutting line for Small size

BODY
Cut 1 from poster board

Apply glue to edges of fabric at each end of tube and to ends of wire. Pinch and gather fabric around ends of wire, holding in place with small elastic bands until glue dries. Center arms across back of figure just below neck, hiding sleeve seam under arm. Glue in place. When glue is dry, bend arms around to front of figure. Trim away any threads or frayed edges of fabric.

5. **Hair:** Fluff up the fleece. Run a line of glue around the hairline and over top of head. Cover with fleece. Press into place. Tie remaining length of ribbon into a small bow and glue to top of head.

6. **Music book:** Cut a small rectangle of white paper and fold in half in shape of a book. Draw staff lines and musical notes. Glue to hands. If desired, glue a birthday candle to hands instead.

A Toy Soldier Story

DESIGNS BY MARY CORCORAN

Adopt a "toy soldier" motif as your holiday theme and make your Christmas decorating extra special. The merry little soldier band is easy to make and makes a wonderfully whimsical display on a mantel or tabletop. Diminutive clothespeg soldiers can decorate a tree or hang from boughs arranged in a large drum for a table centerpiece. Miniature drums are perfect surprise containers for candy and nuts, and match the little napkin rings. Tuck crepe paper soldier hats inside your own Christmas crackers and you have a complete holiday table setting.

Toy Soldier

To enlarge feet pattern, see General Directions (page 130).

YOU NEED

- **Red felt as follows:**

    8 x 3 1/8 in. (20.5 x 8.0 cm), for jacket

    two pieces, each 3 1/2 x 1 in. (9.0 x 2.5 cm), for sleeves

    two circles, each 3/8 in. (1.0 cm) in diameter, for cheeks

- **Black felt as follows:**

    9 x 5 1/2 in. (23.0 x 14.0 cm), for legs

    3 in. (7.5 cm) square, for feet

    8 x 1/4 in. (20.5 x 0.6 cm), for belt

- Piece of pink felt, 2 1/2 x 3/4 in. (6.5 x 2.0 cm), for hands

- Piece of black fake fur, 7 1/4 x 4 in. (18.5 x 10.0 cm), for hat

- Piece of pink cotton broadcloth, 7 x 4 in. (18.0 x 10.0 cm), for head

- Matching threads

- 3/8 yd. (0.30 m) gold ribbon, 1/8 in. (0.3 cm) wide

- 1/4 yd. (0.20 m) gold braid, 3/8 in. (1.0 cm) wide

- Two tiny black beads

- Six tiny gold beads

- Polyester fiberfill

- Scotchgard

- Red felt-tip permanent marker

- Piece of black Bristol board, 3 in. (approx. 7.5 cm) square

- White craft glue

- Dressmaker's chalk pencil

- Brown paper

1. **Head:** Following manufacturer's directions, spray pink broadcloth with Scotchgard. This will prevent facial features from running. Fold in half so right sides are together and short ends meet. Using a 1/4 in. (0.6 cm) seam allowance, stitch seam opposite the fold. Run a line of gathering stitches around both raw edges. Gather one end tightly. Knot threads. Turn right-side out. Stuff head firmly with small amounts of fiberfill to within 1/2 in. (1.3 cm) of open end. Gather, leaving a small opening. Knot threads. Stuff small pieces of fiberfill through hole into head to smooth out any wrinkles. Seam should be at side of head. Referring to photo, draw face on lower half of head with red marker. Using black thread, sew on black beads for eyes. Glue on red felt cheeks.

2. **Legs:** Fold leg piece in half so short ends meet. Stitch seam opposite fold. Turn right-side out. Seam becomes center front. Pin this seam to center back line. Stitch down center. Stuff legs lightly. Cut two 3 1/2 in. (9.0 cm) lengths of gold ribbon. Glue these up side of each leg.

3. Place head on top of legs and slipstitch in place.

4. **Jacket:** Round off bottom corners of jacket piece as shown in Diagram. With top edges even, glue or sew one end of each sleeve to top edge of jacket as shown in Diagram. Cut two lengths of gold braid and two lengths of ribbon, each 1 in. (2.5 cm) long. Glue braid across top of sleeves, and ribbon across bottom of

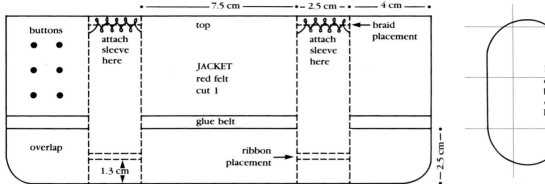
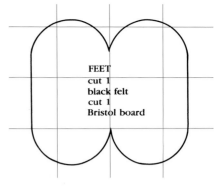

sleeves, where indicated. With red thread, sew on six gold beads for buttons. Wrap jacket around upper half of soldier's body and overlap at front. Glue. Pin in place until glue dries. Glue belt around waist. Cut small piece of braid for buckle and glue to center front of belt.

5. **Hands:** Fold pink felt in half so short ends meet. Cut along fold and round off corners at one end of each hand. Glue one hand under bottom edge of each sleeve, allowing 1/2 in. (1.3 cm) of hand to show below sleeves.

6. **Hat:** Fold piece of fake fur in half so right sides are together and short edges meet. Stitch up this seam and along one end. Turn right-side out. Fit hat on soldier's head, positioning seam at side of head. For strap, wrap remaining length of braid under chin and tuck ends under hat on either side of head. Trim and glue ends in place.

7. **Feet:** Glue black felt square to Bristol board. Cut out feet. Check soldier's balance. Poke more stuffing into legs, if necessary. Glue bottom of legs to center of feet.

Peg Soldier Ornament

PEG SOLDIER
FACE

YOU NEED

- **Piece of red felt, 2 x 1/4 in. (5.0 cm x 0.6 cm)**
- **Scrap of black felt**
- **3/4 in. (2.0 cm) gold braid, 3/8 in. (1.0 cm) wide**
- **1 1/4 in. (3.2 cm) gold cord, 1/16 in. (0.2 cm) wide**
- **Gold thread**
- **5 1/2 yd. (5.00 m) medium-weight black yarn**
- **Springless wooden clothespeg**
- **Three tiny gold beads**
- **Red, black and white acrylic paint**
- **Fine and medium artist's paintbrushes**
- **Black and red felt-tip permanent markers**
- **Piece of cardboard, 2 1/2 x 3/4 in. (6.5 x 2.0 cm)**
- **White craft glue**

1. Paint knob on top of peg white, for head. Paint bottom 2 1/8 in. (5.5 cm) black, for pants, and middle section red, for jacket. Let dry. Mix red and white paint to make pink. Referring to Diagram, paint pink cheeks and draw eyes and mouth with markers.

2. Cut red felt in half so you have two arms, 1 in. (2.5 cm) long. Cut two 1/4 in. (0.6 cm) squares of black felt for hands. Round off corner on one end of each hand. Glue opposite end of hands to bottom of each arm. Glue arms to either side of peg, 1/4 in. down from neck.

3. Cut gold braid in half and glue one piece across each shoulder. Glue three beads down front of jacket, 1/4 in. (0.6 cm) apart. Glue gold cord under chin and up either side of face.

4. **Hat:** Thread darning needle with 12 in. (30.0 cm) length of yarn. Fold so doubled. Wrap remaining yarn around width of cardboard. Slip needle under wrapped yarn on one side of cardboard. Gather up and tie as tightly as possible. Slide yarn off cardboard. Cut loops. Trim pom-pom into oval shape of bearskin hat. Glue on top of head.

5. Thread a hanging loop of gold thread through top of hat.

Graham Wafer Sentry Box

YOU NEED

- **Two egg whites**
- **1 tsp (5 mL) lemon juice**
- **Approx. 3 cups (750 mL) icing sugar**
- **Graham wafers (the kind that are almost square — one 1 lb. (500 g) package makes two sentry boxes)**
- **Granulated sugar**
- **Assorted candies such as jelly beans, cinnamon hearts and candy canes**
- **Baking sheet**
- **Large skillet (electric works best)**
- **Serrated-edged knife**
- **Piping bag and plain tip or a cone made from parchment or heavy waxed paper**
- **Wooden spoon**

TO MAKE ROYAL ICING:

Beat egg whites with lemon juice until stiff peaks form. Gradually beat in icing sugar until mixture is of spreading consistency, or until knife drawn through leaves a clean, sharp line. Fill bag or cone three-quarters full, pushing icing into tip. Close wide end, folding sides toward middle and rolling top down to level of icing. Cover extra icing with a damp cloth to keep it from drying out. Keep at room temperature while building sentry box.

TO ASSEMBLE:

1. **Edible glue:** Put a 1/2 in. (1.3 cm) layer of sugar in skillet. Heat, stirring with wooden spoon over medium-high heat until sugar melts. Reduce heat to keep melted sugar liquid (not tacky). This makes a quick-hardening edible glue, but it is extremely hot. Caution: Do not touch or taste!

2. Arrange wafers (bumpy-side down) on baking sheet in groups as shown in Diagram 1. Long side of wafer is width of sentry box, short side is the height. Rub all adjoining wafers together. This "sanding" gives edges a smoother finish for joining.

3. Glue each grouping together as follows: Dip one edge of wafer into hot syrup and glue it firmly to its neighbor on baking sheet. Keep dipped side of wafer down when lifting it from skillet, so glue doesn't touch skin. For large groupings, attach pairs of wafers together, then join pairs to each other.

4. Working on baking sheet, join sides to back so you have a three-sided building.

5. With serrated-edged knife, gently saw roof in half. Dip one short edge of each roof piece into syrup. Glue these to top edge of sides of sentry box, leaning pieces in toward center to form peaked roof. Any gap along peak of roof will be hidden later with icing.

6. Gently saw peak from point A to points B on both sides (see Diagram 2). Large triangle is back peak. Discard one small triangle. Remaining small triangle is front peak. Glue front and back peaks in place along outer edges of roof. Gaps will be hidden later with icing.

TO DECORATE:

If using paper cone, cut off tip so icing will flow freely. Hold cone in left hand and wrap fingers of right hand around folds of cone (opposite for lefties). Direct cone to area to be iced, then squeeze. Keep icing in tip, near wafer. Using a zigzag pattern, ice over every seam. Decorate as desired, using icing and candies.

Let icing harden for about 24 hours in a dry place. Remove sentry box from cookie sheet and display in a dry place. If you want to preserve it for next Christmas, carefully pack it in a plastic bag and freeze, or spray it with several coats of urethane, wrap well in plastic and store in a dry place.

Diagram 1

| SIDE | BACK | SIDE | ROOF |

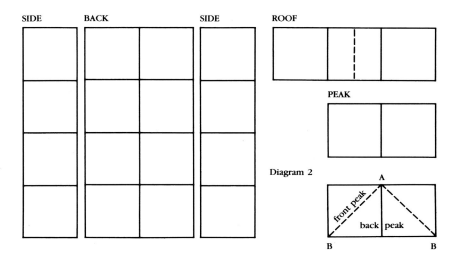

PEAK

Diagram 2

Little Drummer

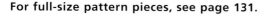

For full-size pattern pieces, see page 131.

1. **Body:** Fold cotton in half so right sides are together and short edges meet. Trace around body pattern onto doubled fabric. Stitch along drawn line, leaving open at bottom where indicated. Cut out body, leaving a 1/4 in. (0.6 cm) seam allowance around all edges. Clip curves. Turn right-side out. Stuff firmly. Slipstitch opening closed.

2. **Face:** Using running stitch, sew pink felt face to body, 1/4 in. (0.6 cm) below seam at top of head. Using three strands of black floss, embroider French knots for eyes. Embroider red mouth in stem stitch. Color cheeks with red pencil.

3. **Pants:** Wrap pants around lower half of body and overlap at center front. Slipstitch in place. Cut two

1 1/2 in. (3.8 cm) lengths of gold ribbon. Glue these up side of each leg.

4. **Jacket:** Wrap jacket around upper half of body just below face and overlap at center front. Slipstitch in place. Glue or sew one end of each sleeve to top edge on either side of jacket. Cut two lengths of gold braid and two lengths of ribbon, each 5/8 in. (1.5 cm) long. Glue braid across top of sleeves and ribbon across bottom of sleeves, 1/8 in. (0.3 cm) from edge. With gold thread, sew three gold beads for buttons down jacket front, 1/4 in. (0.6 cm) to left of center, and another three to right of center. Thread a loop of gold thread between two top buttons. Do the same between the two other pairs of parallel buttons. Cut a 3/8 in. (1.0 cm) piece of braid and glue to center front for belt buckle.

5. **Hands:** Fold pink felt in half so short ends meet. Cut along fold and round off corners at one end of each hand. Glue one hand under bottom edge of each sleeve, allowing 1/4 in. (0.6 cm) of hand to show below sleeves.

6. **Hat:** Fold piece of fake fur in half so right sides are together and short edges meet. Stitch up this seam and along one end. Turn right-side out. Fit hat on drummer's head, positioning seam at side of head. For strap, wrap a length of ribbon under chin and tuck ends under hat on either side of head.
Trim and glue ends in place.

7. **Drumsticks:** Cut off points at end of toothpicks. Glue red bead to one end of each toothpick and glue other end under each hand.

8. **Feet:** Cut feet from black felt. Glue to base of drummer.

Drum Bonbon Dish

YOU NEED

- **Piece of black felt, 8 x 3 3/4 in. (20.5 x 9.5 cm)**

- **Piece of red felt, 8 x 1 in. (20.5 x 2.5 cm)**

- **Black Bristol board, cut into the following pieces:**

  7 1/2 x 1 3/4 in. (19.5 x 4.5 cm), for side of drum

  two 3 in. (7.5 cm) squares, for lid and bottom

- **Piece of shiny gold paper, 6 x 3 in. (15.0 x 7.5 cm)**

- **1 yd. (0.90 m) gold cord, 1/16 in. (0.2 cm) wide**

- **Eight gold paper fasteners, size No. 3 (available at office supply stores)**

- **Two red wooden beads, 1/2 in. (1.3 cm) in diameter**

- **Two pieces of 1/8 in. (0.3 cm) dowelling, each 3 in. (7.5 cm) long**

- **Red and black thread**

- **White pencil**

- **Hole punch**

- **White craft glue**

- **Geometry compass**

---

1. Using white pencil and referring to Diagram, draw placement of holes on Bristol board side piece. Punch holes. Run board over sharp table edge so it curves to form a circle. Dab glue on outer surface. Center and glue to black felt, allowing 1 in. (2.5 cm) felt overlap on long edges and 1/4 in. (0.6 cm) overlap at ends.

2. Poke tip of scissors blade through punched holes into felt. Insert paper fasteners from felt side and open ends on wrong side to secure. Glue strip of red felt down center of black felt between fasteners. Fold felt overlaps to inside, covering backs of fasteners. Glue in place.

3. Leaving a 9 in. (23.0 cm) length of gold cord free at beginning, wrap cord around fastener at one end of drum. Carry it diagonally across to next fastener on opposite side, and so on, in zigzag fashion around all fasteners. Do not cut off extra cord.

4. Curve side piece up to form a tube and slipstitch ends together. Wrap extra cord around first fastener to complete zigzag formation.

5. Using compass and white pencil, draw two 2 1/2 in. (6.0 cm) diameter circles on squares of black Bristol board. Cut out. From gold paper, cut two circles, each 1/8 in. (0.3 cm) larger than Bristol board circles. Glue these to both sides of one Bristol board circle (lid). Punch hole close to edge of lid. Thread loose cord through hole and knot loosely to hold lid in place. Fit remaining circle into bottom of drum, trimming to fit if necessary.

6. To make drumsticks, glue a bead to one end of each dowel. Let dry. Slip drumsticks through knot on lid. Tighten knot and tie cord in a bow.

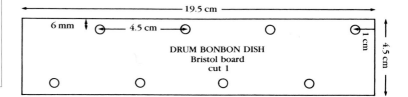

DRUM BONBON DISH
Bristol board
cut 1

Drum Napkin Ring

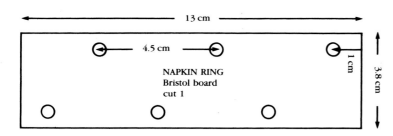

1. Referring to Napkin Ring Diagram, follow Step 1 of Drum Bonbon Dish (page 33), allowing a 7/8 in. (2.2 cm) felt overlap on long edges.

2. Complete as for Drum Bonbon Dish (page 33) Steps 2 to 4, but leave a 2 in. (5.0 cm) end of cord at beginning of zigzag pattern. Glue ends of cord around fastener and trim.

13 cm

4.5 cm

1 cm

3.8 cm

NAPKIN RING
Bristol board
cut 1

Drum Centerpiece

1. Cut Bristol board in half lengthwise. Set one strip aside. On other strip, measure and mark a line 5 in. (12.5 cm) from one end. This is the overlap. Run board over sharp table edge so it curves to form a circle. Overlap ends forming a tube. Glue, holding in place with paper clips until dry.

2. Spread glue around outer rims of drum. Center and wrap black felt around drum, overlapping at seam. Glue overlap. Dab glue along long edges of red felt strip and wrap around center of black felt. Glue overlap.

3. Mark positions for three buttons evenly spaced, approx. 5 3/4 in. (14.5 cm) apart, around bottom of

drum, 1/2 in. (1.3 cm) from rim of Bristol board, placing first button close to seam. Sew buttons in place through Bristol board and felt. Sew three buttons around top rim in same manner, spacing them midway between the bottom ones.

4. To reinforce drum, glue second strip of Bristol board inside drum. Glue felt overlaps to inside at top and bottom.

5. Cut ribbon in half. Glue each piece around drum along edges of red felt strip, overlapping ends at seam.

6. Starting at seam, thread cord around buttons as for Drum Bonbon Dish, page 33. Knot ends together. Trim.

7. Fill flowerpot with gravel, and arrange branches in it. Place pot inside drum.

Christmas Crackers

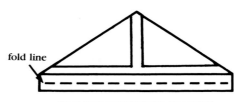

HAT FOR CHRISTMAS CRACKER

TO MAKE HAT:

1. Fold one sheet of tissue paper in half lengthwise. Run finger along crease. Open out and lay flat. Fold in half widthwise. Fold corners at each end of fold, down to center line, forming peak.

2. Fold one layer of tissue at bottom of hat up to meet bottom edge of peak (see Diagram). Fold up the same again. Repeat for brim on other side. To hold brim together, dab glue on inside of brim at front and back of hat.

3. **Cockade:** Cut a piece of contrasting colored tissue paper, 15 x 9 in. (38.0 x 23.0 cm). Fold in half lengthwise. Fold in half widthwise repeatedly until piece measures approx. 4 1/2 x 1 in. (11.5 x 2.5 cm). Cut fringe along raw edge every 1/4 in. (0.6 cm) to a depth of 4 in. (10 cm). Do not unfold. Tuck base of cockade 1/2 in. (1.3 cm) under brim on one side of hat. Glue notary seal over brim and cockade to hold in place.

4. Fold up hat so it will fit into toilet paper roll.

TO MAKE CRACKER:

1. Stuff toilet paper roll with snapper, hat, favor and joke.

2. Cut two 10 in. (25.5 cm) squares of red crepe paper. Wrap both layers around roll (so roll runs along grain of

YOU NEED

For each cracker:

- **Two sheets of tissue paper in contrasting colors**
- **Red crepe paper (one package makes approx. nine crackers)**
- **Piece of gold foil paper, 7 x 3 1/2 in. (18.0 x 9.0 cm)**
- **Piece of black crepe paper, 7 x 2 1/2 in. (18.0 x 6.5 cm)**
- **Two gold notary seals**

(available at office supply stores)√√

- **3/4 yd. (0.70 m) gold cord, 1/16 in. (0.2 cm) wide**
- **Toilet paper roll**
- **One snapper, 11 in. (28.0 cm) long**
- **Small favor to fit inside roll**
- **One-line saying, joke or fortune**
- **White craft glue**

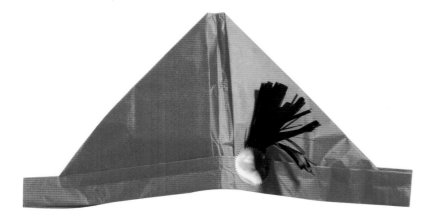

TO MAKE HAT:

1. Fold one sheet of tissue paper in half lengthwise. Run finger along crease. Open out and lay flat. Fold in half widthwise. Fold corners at each end of fold, down to center line, forming peak.

2. Fold one layer of tissue at bottom of hat up to meet bottom edge of peak (see Diagram). Fold up the same again. Repeat for brim on other side. To hold brim together, dab glue on inside of brim at front and back of hat.

3. **Cockade:** Cut a piece of contrasting colored tissue paper, 15 x 9 in. (38.0 x 23.0 cm). Fold in half lengthwise. Fold in half widthwise repeatedly until

Merry Mouse Choir

DESIGN BY CAROLYN SMITH

'Twas the night before Christmas/Church bells had stopped ringing/
Most folks were asleep/But the mice were still singing...

Stitched from bits of felt, broadcloth and eyelet, and complete with little songbooks, this delightful mouse chorus looks great on a mantel or as a table decoration.

YOU NEED

For each mouse:

- Piece of gray felt, 9 x 6 in. (23.0 x 15.0 cm)
- Scrap of red felt, 2 x 1 in. (5.0 x 2.5 cm)
- Piece of red broadcloth, 6 1/4 x 4 1/2 (16 x 11.5 cm)
- 1/4 yd. (0.20 m) flat eyelet lace, 3 in. (7.5 cm) wide
- Matching threads

- Gray buttonhole twist thread, for whiskers
- Two black beads, for eyes
- Polyester fiberfill
- Piece of white paper, 2 x 1 in. (5.0 x 2.5 cm)
- Black fine-tip permanent marker
- White craft glue
- Brown paper

For full-size pattern pieces, see page 131.

1. Cut all pieces from gray felt.

2. Using a short running stitch, sew head/body pieces together close to outer edge, leaving open at bottom. Stitching will show on right side. Make a 1/4 in. (0.6 cm) slit for ears on each side of head as indicated. Roll ear piece lengthwise and push through one ear slit and out the other. Stuff head/body with small amounts of fiberfill, adjusting ears if necessary. Stitch base to bottom of body.

3. Sew on bead eyes. Thread a needle with gray thread for whiskers. Push needle through snout from one side to the other. Cut thread leaving a 3/4 in. (2.0 cm) whisker on each side of snout. Thread through two more sets of whiskers in same manner. Stiffen whiskers with clear nail polish if desired.

4. **Choir gown:** Turn under 1/4 in. (0.6 cm) on one long edge and both short edges of red fabric. Hem. Turn under approx. 1/2 in. (1.3 cm) on remaining raw edge (neck edge). Check length on mouse and adjust if necessary. Run a line of gathering stitches around neck, 3/8 in. (1.0 cm) from folded edge. Pull up thread to fit around mouse's neck. Knot ends. Fit gown on mouse, positioning opening at back. Slipstitch top half of back opening closed.

5. **Surplice:** Locate center point along length of eyelet lace. Measure and mark points 1 in. (2.5 cm) to either side of center and 2 in. (5.0 cm) up from finished edge. Make a 1/4 in. (0.6 cm) slit at these two points. Slip straight end of paw through each slit and slipstitch in place on wrong side of eyelet. Turn under 1/4 in. (0.6 cm), then 1/4 in. (0.6 cm) again on both ends of eyelet. Hem. Turn under 1/4 in. (0.6 cm) along remaining raw edge (neck edge) of eyelet. Run a line of gathering stitches around neck close to fold. Fit surplice on mouse, positioning opening at back. Adjust gathers to fit around neck. Knot ends. Slipstitch edges together at neck.

6. **Hymn book:** With black marker, draw musical notes on one side of piece of paper. Glue to scrap of red felt and bend in half to form book. Glue book between paws.

7. Stitch straight end of tail to base at center back. Stitch remaining paws to base on either side of center front.

CHAPTER 2

Tree Trims

Nutcracker Ornaments

DESIGNS BY RENÉE SCHWARZ

Set a magical mood with tree trims inspired by The Nutcracker. *Tiny felt ornaments such as Toy Soldier, Drum, Mouse and Ballet Slippers will bring the wonder of this famous ballet into your home during the Christmas season*

Felt Toy Soldier Ornament

Finished ornament is 6 1/4 in. (approx. 16.0 cm) tall.

YOU NEED

- Piece of flesh-tone cotton or unbleached muslin, 4 x 2 1/2 in. (10.0 x 6.0 cm)
- Scrap of black felt, 5 1/2 x 4 3/4 in. (13.0 x 12.0 cm), for hat and boots
- Scrap of royal blue felt, 4 x 2 1/2 in. (10.0 x 6.0 cm), for pants
- Scrap of red felt, 4 3/4 x 2 3/4 in. (12.0 x 7.0 cm), for shirt
- Scrap of white felt, 3 1/2 x 2 in. (8.0 x 5.0 cm), for hands, cross and brush
- 6 1/4 in. (approx. 16.0 cm) gold braid, 1/8 in. (0.3 cm) wide
- 5 1/2 in. (approx. 14.0 cm) flat gold braid, 3/8 in. (0.9 cm) wide
- Matching threads
- Invisible nylon thread
- Small amount polyester fiberfill
- Navy, black, brown and red acrylic or fabric paint or embroidery floss
- White craft glue
- Brown paper

For full-size pattern pieces, see page 133.

1. **Head:** From flesh-tone cotton, cut two heads. With right sides together and using a 1/4 in. (0.6 cm) seam allowance, sew heads together, leaving open at top. Turn right-side out. Stuff. Slipstitch opening closed. Paint or embroider navy eyes, red cheeks, brown nose and chin and black moustache.

2. **Body:** From red felt, cut two shirts. From blue felt, cut two pants. From black felt, cut two boots. From white felt, cut two hands and one cross. Overlap top edge of boot 1/4 in. (0.6 cm) over bottom edge of pants. Edgestitch in place. Repeat with other boot and pants pieces. Place boots/pants pieces wrong sides together, and edgestitch boots together around outside edge. Topstitch down center of boots. Stuff. Overlap bottom edge of shirt 1/4 in. over top edge of pants. Edgestitch in place. Repeat with other shirt piece on other side of pants. Edgestitch pants together down outside edges. Topstitch up center of pants from boots to 3/8 in. (1.0 cm) from shirt. Place hands between shirt sleeves so they project 3/8 in. beyond cuff. Edgestitch shirt together around outside edges, leaving open at neck. Stuff body. Insert neck into shirt neck opening. Edgestitch in place by hand. Glue cross onto front of shirt.

3. **Hat:** From black felt, cut two hats and from white felt, cut one brush. With right sides together and using a 1/4 in. (0.6 cm) seam allowance, sew hat pieces together, leaving bottom edge open. Turn right side out. Stuff lightly. Turn under 1/8 in. (0.3 cm) around bottom edge. Pin to head. Sew base of brush to center front of hat. Tie a double knot in center of narrow gold braid and hand-stitch this knot in place over base of brush. Bring ends of braid around to back of head and tuck under hat. Slipstitch hat in place, catching braid ends in stitching.

4. Sew 3 1/2 in. (approx. 9.0 cm) length of wide gold braid around waist, overlapping and turning under ends at back. Cut two 1 in. (2.5 cm) lengths of wide gold braid for epaulettes. Fold ends under and hand-stitch to each shoulder.

5. Thread hanging loop of invisible thread through top of hat.

A Felt Toy Soldier Ornament to charm the young and young at heart.

Felt Mouse Ornament

Finished ornament is 4 in. (approx. 10.0 cm) tall.

YOU NEED

- Piece of gray felt, 11 x 5 in. (28.0 x 12.0 cm)
- Small scrap of black felt
- 5 1/2 in. (approx. 14.0 cm) silver cord, 1/8 in. (0.3 cm) wide
- Matching thread
- Invisible nylon thread
- Black buttonhole twist thread
- Black embroidery floss
- Small amount polyester fiberfill
- 4 in. (approx. 10.5 cm) thin wire, approx. 1/32 in. (0.1 cm) thick
- No. 22 tapestry needle, for sword
- Brown paper

For full-size pattern pieces, see page 133.

1. **Head:** From gray felt, cut one head and a rectangle approx. 2 3/4 x 2 1/2 in. (7.0 x 6.0 cm). Place cutout head on rectangle and edgestitch pieces together around outside edge of head, leaving open between ears. Trim rectangle to shape of head. Stuff lightly. Edgestitch opening closed. Using two strands of floss and satin stitch, embroider eyes and nose. Thread two lengths of buttonhole thread through snout for whiskers. Trim.

2. **Body:** From gray felt, cut one body and a rectangle approx. 4 1/2 x 3 1/2 in. (11.0 x 9.0 cm). Edgestitch cutout body to rectangle (leaving opening at neck), trim felt, stuff and close opening as for head. Hand-stitch head to front of body at neck.

3. **Tail:** From gray felt, cut a strip 4 3/4 x 1 1/8 in. (12.0 x 3.0 cm). Fold strip in half lengthwise over wire. Making sure that wire is enclosed in the fold, stitch long edges together 3/16 in. (approx. 0.4 cm) from fold, ending stitching in a point 1/4 in. (0.6 cm) from one end. Trim felt to 1/8 in. (0.3 cm) from seam. Bend tail into S shape and stitch open end to middle of mouse's back, 1 1/8 in. (approx. 3.0 cm) up from bottom of feet. Fold silver cord in half to form a loop. Sew together 3/8 in. (1.0 cm) from ends. Slip loop diagonally over mouse's shoulder.

4. **Sword:** Sew tapestry needle to palm of mouse's left hand, stitching through eye of needle. Fold hand over eye of needle and stitch in place. Cut a 1/2 in. (1.3 cm) diameter circle from black felt. Slip circle onto sword and attach to top of hand with a dab of glue.

5. Thread hanging loop of invisible thread through top of head.

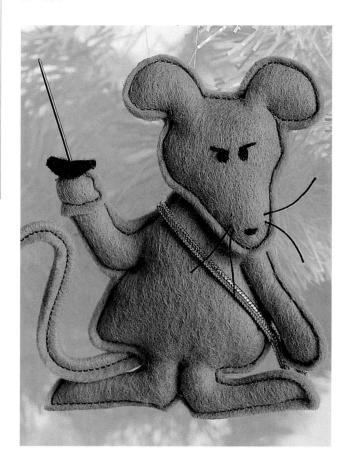

Felt Drum Ornament

Finished ornament is 3 1/4 x 3 in. (approx. 8.0 x 7.5 cm).

YOU NEED

- Piece of white felt, 7 x 3 1/2 in. (18.0 x 9.0 cm)
- Piece of red felt, 4 x 3 1/2 in. (10.0 x 9.0 cm)
- 3/4 yd. (0.70 m) gold braid, 1/8 in. (0.3 cm) wide
- Matching threads
- Small amount polyester fiberfill
- Brown paper

For full-size pattern pieces, see page 134.

1. From white felt, cut two drums, and from red felt, cut four bands.

2. Position gold braid along zigzag broken lines on each drum piece, tacking in place at each corner. On each drum piece, position one band so lower edge extends 1/4 in. (0.6 cm) below bottom edge of drum and another band the same way up at top edge of drum, having top corners matching. Edgestitch upper edge of bottom band and both long edges of top band in place on each drum.

3. Pin decorated drum pieces wrong sides together. Cut a 8 1/4 in. (21.0 cm) length of braid. Sandwich ends between felt at top corners of drum, forming a handle. Changing thread color where appropriate, edgestitch drum pieces together around outside edges, leaving a small opening along one side. Stuff lightly. Edgestitch opening closed.

Felt Ballet Slippers Ornament

Finished ornament is 4 3/4 x 4 3/8 in. (approx. 12.0 x 11.0 cm).

YOU NEED
• Piece of white felt, 16 1/2 x 7 in. (42.0 x 18.0 cm) • 1 3/4 yd. (1.60 m) satin ribbon, 3/8 in. (0.9 cm) wide	• Two small gold bows • Matching thread • Small amount polyester fiberfill • Brown paper

For full-size pattern, see page 133.

1. From felt, cut three slipper pieces. Cut inside oval-shaped section out of two (for shoe upper) of these three pieces.

2. Pin two shoe upper pieces together. Edgestitch, then satin-stitch around edge of center cutout. Insert a small amount of fiberfill between the two layers. With right sides together, pin upper to remaining piece (slipper sole). Stitch together using a 1/4 in. (0.6 cm) seam allowance. Turn right-side out.

3. Cut two 15 3/4 in. (40.0 cm) lengths of ribbon. Sew one end of each to inside side edges of slipper. Sew bow on top front of slipper.

4. Make a second slipper in same manner, following Steps 1 to 3. Knot and tie loose ends of ribbons from each slipper together in a bow. Stitch through knot to secure. To hold slippers together as a pair, tack sides together.

Angelic Ornaments

Each of these four heavenly ornaments has a personality of its own. Angelica has a mop of orange hair, feathery wings and a magic wand. Mini Angel is a miniature felt version of the heirloom Treetop Angel (page 68). Angel Fluff may very well be the tiniest ornament on your tree. And for anyone who likes to work with wood, Cheeky Little Angel is a whimsical charmer. All are guaranteed to capture everyone's heart.

Angelica

Design by Joan Doherty

YOU NEED

- **Piece of white cotton broadcloth, 12 x 6 in. (30.0 x 15.0 cm)**
- **Piece of pink felt, 3 1/4 in. (8.0 cm) square**
- **Scrap of red felt**
- **Blue, black, brown, red and pink liquid embroidery**
- **Small amount of fleece, dyed orange or yellow (available at weaving stores)**
- **Matching threads**
- **Invisible nylon thread**
- **Two white feathers, approx. 3 in. (8.0 cm) long**
- **Gold tinsel wire, 5 1/2 in. (14.0 cm) long**
- **Gold glitter**
- **Gold paint**
- **Little bunch of tiny artificial flowers**
- **Polyester fiberfill**
- **Toothpick, for wand**
- **Piece of cardboard, 2 in. (5.0 cm) square**
- **White craft glue**
- **Brown paper**

For full-size pattern pieces, see page 132.

1. Cut two angel bodies from broadcloth, adding a 1/4 in. (0.6 cm) seam allowance on all edges. From pink felt, cut one face and two hands. From red felt, cut one heart.

2. Using a narrow zigzag stitch, appliqué face to right side of one body piece. With liquid embroidery, draw blue eyes with black pupils, brown eyebrows and nostrils, red mouth and pink cheeks.

3. With right sides together, sew body front to back around curved edge, using a 1/4 in. (0.6 cm) seam allowance. Turn right-side out. Stuff firmly. Turn under 1/4 in. around bottom edge and slipstitch closed.

4. Arrange fleece hair on angel's head. Bend gold tinsel wire around hair to look like a halo. Tack hair and halo in place on each side of head. Stick flowers into halo on one side of head.

5. From cardboard, cut one star. Glue end of toothpick to star, for wand. Cover both sides of star with glue and dip in glitter. Let dry. Paint toothpick gold. Let dry. Sew wand to front of angel with a few tiny stitches. Glue hands over wand, hiding the stitches. Glue heart in place.

6. Poke feathers in back of angel. Thread a hanging loop of invisible thread through top of head.

Mini Angel

Design by Carol Schmidt

This is the miniature version of the Treetop Angel on page 68.

YOU NEED

- **Piece of white felt, 6 1/4 x 4 3/4 in. (16.0 x 12.0 cm)**
- **Scrap of flesh-tone felt**
- **Crocheted doily, approx. 3 1/2 in. (9.0 cm) in diameter**
- **4 in. (10.0 cm) white lace, 3/8 in. (1.0 cm) wide**
- **White thread**
- **Brown and red embroidery floss**
- **Gold embroidery thread such as DMC Fil Or**
- **No. 8 white DMC Coton Perlé**
- **Polyester fiberfill**
- **Small artist's paintbrush**
- **Powder blush**

For full-size pattern, see page 134.

1. From white felt, cut two angel bodies. From flesh-tone felt, cut face and hands.

2. Sew face and hands to front body using tiny backstitches. With one strand of floss and using small outline stitches, embroider brown eyes and red mouth. With white Coton Perlé, embroider 1/8 in. (0.3 cm) long backstitches up center front and around yoke area on each side of hands. Starting at bottom, lace gold thread in and out of backstitches up one side to face. Embroider French knots around face, for hair, wrapping thread twice around needle for each knot. Continue lacing thread down backstitches on opposite side. With gold thread, embroider one flower on each side of front, using detached chain or lazy daisy stitch for petals and French knot for center.

3. With right sides together, sew front to back using a 1/4 in. (0.6 cm) seam allowance and leaving open at bottom. Clip curves. Turn right-side out. Stuff lightly. Turn under 1/4 in. around bottom edge. Baste lace along inside of bottom edge, turning raw ends toward back. Backstitch opening closed.

4. Fold doily in half and tack to back of angel for wings. Using paintbrush, highlight cheeks with a little blush.

5. Thread hanging loop of gold thread through top of angel.

Cheeky Little Angel

Design by Jane Buckles

YOU NEED

- **Scraps of pine, 1 x 6 x 6 in. (2.5 x 15.0 x 15.0 cm) and 1/2 x 5/8 x 2 1/2 in. (1.3 x 1.5 x 6.5 cm)**
- **3/8 in. (1.0 cm) dowelling, 4 in. (10.0 cm) long**
- **1/8 in. (0.3 cm) dowelling, 4 in. (10.0 cm) long**
- **4 3/4 in. (12.0 cm) coat hanger wire, for halo**
- **1 1/4 yd. (1.10 m) orange craft yarn, for hair**
- **White craft glue**
- **Flesh-tone, red and blue colored pencils**
- **Black fine-tip permanent marker**
- **White and gold paint**
- **Electric drill with 1/8 in. (3.175 mm) and 3/16 in. (4.763 mm) bits**
- **Band or jigsaw**
- **Hand saw**
- **Sandpaper**
- **Pliers**
- **Screw eye**

1. Transfer angel outline (shown actual size on page 132) onto large piece of pine. Using band or jigsaw, cut out shape. Cut remaining scrap of pine into two pieces, each 1/2 x 5/8 x 1 1/4 in. (1.3 x 1.5 x 3.2 cm), for feet. Cut 3/8 in. (1.0 cm) dowelling into two pieces, each 2 in. (5.0) long, for legs, and then cut 1/8 in. (0.3 cm) dowelling into one piece, 2 1/2 in. (6.0 cm) long, for leg pin, and two pieces, 3/4 in. (2.0 cm) long, for foot pins. Sand all pieces lightly.

2. Drill 1/8 in. (3.175 mm) holes for leg pin, horizontally straight through bottom of body, as shown. Drill 3/16 in. (4.763 mm) holes for leg pin horizontally through top of each leg, 3/16 in. from end. Drill 1/8 in. hole in bottom of each leg and in top of each foot, as shown. Drill fifteen 1/8 in. holes in top of head to accommodate hair and halo.

3. Bend one end of wire into a 1 in. (2.5 cm) diameter circle. Bend other end straight down to form stem of halo.

4. Color face with flesh-tone colored pencil. Paint body and feet white. When dry, transfer wing and arm markings; then paint gold. Paint legs and halo gold. Draw facial features with black marker, and color in eyes with blue pencil and cheeks and mouth with red.

5. Apply glue in horizontal holes at bottom of body. Thread leg pin from one side of body, through outer hole, through hole in one leg, through middle hole, through hole in other leg and then out through outer hole. Legs should move freely. Glue foot pins into bottom of legs and into holes in feet.

6. Insert screw eye into top of head, and glue stem of halo into one of the holes in center top of head.

7. Cut yarn into thirteen pieces. Fold each piece in half. Dab glue on fold and poke into remaining holes in head with a nail or darning needle. When glue is dry, trim hair. Attach hanging thread or ribbon to screw eye.

Movable legs make Cheeky Little Angel a unique ornament. Make several for a heavenly tree.

Angel Fluff

Design by Louise Chisholm

YOU NEED

- **2 3/8 in. (6.0 cm) circle of white cotton fabric**
- **4 3/4 in. (12.0 cm) white eyelet lace, 1 in. (2.5 cm) wide**
- **1 3/8 yd. (1.25 m) gold thread**
- **White thread**
- **Small amounts of blue, gold and pink embroidery floss**
- **Small amount of polyester fiberfill**
- **Two small white feathers**
- **One white plastic flower stamen**

ANGEL FLUFF

FACE (actual size)

1. Transfer face (shown actual size, below) onto center of fabric circle. Using two strands of floss, embroider blue eyes, gold eyebrows and pink nose and mouth.

2. Run a line of gathering stitches around edge of circle. Place small amount of fiberfill on wrong side. Pull up gathering thread as tightly as possible and secure.

3. Fold stamen into a V for arms and stitch to back of head. Run a line of gathering stitches along straight edge of eyelet lace. Gather into a circle and stitch to back of head.

4. Set aside 6 in. (15.0 cm) of gold thread for hanging loop. Wind remaining gold thread around two ringers. Tie loops in center and stitch to top of head for hair.

5. Poke feathers behind neck on each side of head for wings. Stitch in place. Make a tiny bow from pink floss. Stitch in place at front neck.

6. Thread hanging loop of gold thread through top of eyelet.

Inuit Inspirations

DESIGNS BY ANN BOUFFARD

Sometimes the simplest ideas for tree trims fashion the best theme trees. The figurative drawings of the Inuit are the inspiration for a charming collection of baker's clay ornaments. Make all seven designs for a unique tree.

YOU NEED

- **For baker's clay (12 to 14 ornaments):**
  1 cup (250 mL) all-purpose flour
  1/2 cup (125 mL) salt
  1/2 cup (125 mL) water
- **Black peppercorns**
- **Toothpicks**
- **Paper clip**
- **Wire or hairpins**
- **Small pointed knife**
- **Foil**
- **Spatula**
- **Baking sheet**
- **Polyurethane varnish (optional)**

TO MAKE CLAY:

Mix together ingredients for clay to form a soft dough. Working on a floured board, knead until smooth, about 8 to 10 minutes. Clay is very workable and can be easily bent, pinched or molded into desired shapes. Shape each figure and flatten to between 1/4 in. (0.6 cm) and 1/2 in. (1.3 cm) thickness. To attach pieces, moisten each with a little water. With spatula, lift finished figures onto foil and place on baking sheet. Bake in 250°F (120°C) oven for 4 to 5 hours, or until thoroughly dry. Finish with varnish if desired.

TO SHAPE FIGURES:

BIRD

1. **Body:** Roll a ball of clay 1 1/2 in. (4.0 cm) in diameter. Roll this out into a 4 in. (10.0 cm) teardrop shape with points at both ends. Pinch ends to finer points for tail and beak. Lift head up and push slightly toward back to give bird a chest. Press in peppercorn for eye.

2. **Wing:** Roll a ball of clay 3/4 in. (2.0 cm) in diameter. Roll this out into a 3 in. (7.5 cm) teardrop shape. Attach to body. Curve wing and tail up slightly toward back. With knife, mark feathers on wing.

3. **Claws:** Roll two tiny balls into short lengths. Attach to underside of body and bend tips downward (see photo).

4. Make a small U-shaped loop from wire or hairpin. Moisten and insert into top of bird, slightly forward on body for balance.

OWL

1. **Body:** Roll a 1 1/2 in. (4.0 cm) ball into a 3 in. (7.5 cm) teardrop shape. Flatten with heel of hand to approx. 1/2 in. (1.3 cm) thickness.

2. **Head:** Roll a 3/4 in. (2.0 cm) ball. Flatten and attach to wide end of body. Pinch front of head to form owl face (see photo). Press in peppercorns for eyes. Blend head into body by rubbing area with moistened finger.

3. **Wing:** Roll a 3/4 in. (2.0 cm) ball into a 2 1/2 in. (6.5 cm) teardrop shape. Flatten and attach to body. With knife, mark feathers on wing and body.

4. **Claws:** Roll two pea-size balls into short lengths. Attach to underside of body and bend tips downward.

5. Moisten and insert wire loop into top of head.

WALRUS

1. **Body:** Roll a 1 1/2 in. (4.0 cm) ball into a 4 in. (10.0 cm) teardrop shape. Flatten slightly. Pinch at wide end for neck and at pointed end for base of tail. With knife, slit tail in half and mark indentations.

2. **Head:** Raise head and push slightly toward back (see photo). If head will not stay up, clay is too moist — add flour and try again. Poke holes for snout with toothpick. Press in peppercorns for eyes.

3. **Tusks:** Roll two very tiny teardrop shapes and attach to head on either side of snout.

4. **Fin:** Roll a pea-size ball into a teardrop shape. Attach to lower body; mark indentations with knife.

5. Moisten and insert wire loop into top of body.

BEAR

1. **Body:** Roll a 1 1/2 in. (4.0 cm) ball into a 4 in. (10.0 cm) teardrop shape. Flatten. Pinch pointed end slightly to a finer point for nose. Make cut for mouth.

2. **Legs:** Roll two pea-size balls into 1/2 in. (1.3 cm) lengths. Do not flatten. Attach to underside of body for bottom legs. Roll two 1 in. (2.5 cm) balls into 2 in. (5.0 cm) teardrop shapes for top legs. Flatten slightly and attach to body so they are supported by bottom legs. Bend tips of all legs forward to form paws.

3. **Head:** Press in peppercorns for eye and nose. Make a tiny teardrop shape for ear and attach to head.

4. Moisten and insert wire loop into top of body.

SUNDIAL FACE

Flatten a 2 in. (5.0 cm) ball. Roll seven 1/4 in. (0.6 cm)

balls; flatten and attach these around face. Roll out a long, thin length and attach around sundial face inside circles. Attach tiny pieces of clay for mouth and nose. Mark eyes with knife.

GIRL

1. **Parka:** Roll a 1 1/2 in. (4.0 cm) ball into a 2 1/2 in. (6.5 cm) length, slightly smaller at one end. Flatten slightly.

2. **Head:** Roll a 1/2 in. (1.3 cm) ball, flatten slightly and attach to top of parka (smaller end). Mark eyes with knife. Make a curved mouth by pressing in with small end of paper clip. Attach a tiny ball for nose and two slightly larger balls, flattened, for cheeks.

3. **Hood:** Roll a 1 in. (2.5 cm) ball into a 3 in. (7.5 cm) length; attach around head.

4. **Skirt:** Roll a 3/4 in. (2.0 cm) ball into a 2 in. (5.0 cm) length and attach to bottom of parka. Press with little finger to create ruffle effect.

5. **Boots:** Roll two balls the size of large peas into 1 in. (2.5 cm) lengths. Attach to bottom of skirt and bend tips up to form feet.

6. **Arms:** Roll two 1 in. (2.5 cm) balls into 2 1/2 in. (6.5 cm) lengths, each slightly smaller at one end. Flatten slightly. Attach larger ends to shoulders. Bend arms forward across parka.

7. **Hands:** Roll two pea-size balls, flatten and attach to arms. Make tiny slashes for thumbs.

8. **Trim:** Roll out lengths 1/8 to 1/4 in. (0.3 to 0.6 cm) wide and attach at collar, cuffs, bottom of parka and at top of boots. Mark trim and hood with knife for fur texture effect. With end of paper clip, poke holes down front of boots (see photo). Press peppercorns for buttons.

9. Moisten and insert wire loop into top of head.

BOY

1. Make parka, head and hood as for Girl.

2. **Legs:** Roll two 3/4 in. (2.0 cm) balls into 1 1/2 in. (4.0 cm) lengths, each slightly smaller at one end. Flatten slightly and attach larger ends to bottom of parka. Bend tips up to form feet.

3. **Arms:** Roll two 3/4 in. (2.0 cm) balls into 1 1/2 in. (4.0 cm) lengths, each slightly smaller at one end. Flatten slightly and attach larger ends to shoulders so arms are raised.

4. Make holes down boots, hands and trim as for Girl, adding extra trim down front of parka instead of buttons. Mark trim and hood with knife for fur texture effect.

5. Moisten and insert wire loop into top of head.

Knitted Gingerbread Man

DESIGN BY JEAN SCOBIE

Knit a whole batch of gingerbread men. Then use them to decorate a tree or a special gift, or give them as lovable little toys. They'll look good enough to eat!

YOU NEED

- Small quantity of gingerbread-brown Sayelle or similar-weight yarn
- Scraps of dark brown, white and red yarn
- One pair U.S. size 3 (3.00 mm) needles
- Tapestry needle
- Invisible nylon thread
- Polyester fiberfill

Knitting a gingerbread man is simple. Beginning at the feet, knit a rectangle, shaping at the top for the head. When the body is sewn together and stuffed, the arms and legs are defined by stitching through all layers. Embroidered details are added at the end.

See General Directions (page 130) for knitting abbreviations.

Work in St st throughout.
Cast on 32 sts.
Work 20 rows for legs. Place marker at end of row.
Work 14 rows for upper body. Place marker at end of row to indicate neck.
Work 15 rows for head as follows:

Rows 1-8: Work even in St st.
Row 9: Dec 5 sts evenly across row (27 sts rem).
Row 10: Purl.
Row 11: Dec 5 sts evenly across row (22 sts rem).
Row 12: Purl.

Row 13: Dec 5 sts evenly across row (17 sts rem).
Row 14: Purl.
Row 15: K1 (k2 tog), 8 times.
Draw yarn through rem sts and pull up.

TO FINISH:

1. Sew sides tog to form center back seam.
2. Stuff head. Weave a single strand of matching yarn through neck row. Draw up and tie tightly.

3. Stuff body and sew bottom opening closed, pulling in as much as possible.

4. With matching yarn, define arms by sewing small back stitches through all layers from waist to 2 rows below neck. Define legs in same manner, from bottom edge to just below waistline.

5. Embroider arm outline, ankles, mouth, eyes and buttons with colored yarn.

6. Thread a hanging loop of invisible thread through top of head.

Saucy Santas

DESIGN BY SISTER CATHERINE MARY STRONG

Let children capture the magic of the season with their own little tree. Cone-shaped paper Santas are the perfect project for the kindergarten crowd — with a little help from you.

YOU NEED

- Red construction paper
- White typing paper
- Red felt-tip marker
- Red thread
- White craft glue
- Clothespin
- Needle
- Geometry compass

1. Using compass, draw an 11 1/2 in. (29.0 cm) diameter circle on red construction paper. Cut out. Cut circle into four equal pie-shaped wedges.

2. Using photo as a guide, cut a Santa face and beard from white paper. Draw eyes and mouth. Glue to center of one wedge.

3. Roll up sides of wedge to form a cone, overlapping edges 1/2 in. (1.3 cm). Glue in place. Hold together with clothespin until glue dries.

4. Thread a loop of red thread through tip of cone. Make Santas from three remaining wedges in the same manner.

CHAPTER 3

Family Fun

Festive Roller Printing

DESIGNS BY MARY CORCORAN

Children love to participate in holiday preparations. With easy-to-do roller printing projects, they can create their own practical Christmas presents, cards, decorations and gift wrap. The stencils and rollers are designed to be used on paper and fabric. Make the cheerful Child's Play Smock to keep your little artist's clothes clean.

Printing

YOU NEED

- Small paint roller, approx 3 1/2 in. (9.0 cm) wide
- Pair of shoe insoles (preferably men's size large) with foam rubber backing, with or without perforations, for making patterned roller
- Paper such as newsprint, shelf paper, construction paper, artist's drawing paper, Bristol board or factory cotton (unbleached muslin), depending on the individual project
- Poster paint (tempera)

- for paper printing
- Non-toxic, water-soluble fabric paint for fabric printing
- Paintbrush
- Non-toxic, washable felt-tip markers
- Contact cement
- Toothpick
- Masking tape
- Flat, smooth Styrofoam or foil tray
- Tracing paper
- Newspaper or plastic tablecloth

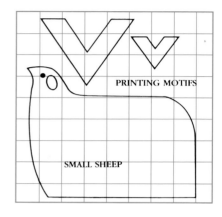

PRINTING MOTIFS

SMALL SHEEP

Note: Printing with a plain roller is very easy and gives a mottled, textured effect. To make a patterned roller requires an adult's help.

TO MAKE PATTERNED ROLLER:

1. Trace small sheep and small or large V motifs (above) onto tracing paper, or design your own motifs. Cut out.

2. Trace around paper patterns onto fabric side of insole. You can use several small motifs on each roller. Cut out carefully.

3. Use toothpick to spread contact cement on fabric side of insole cutouts. Glue these evenly spaced around roller. Be sure to fill the width of the roller.

TO PRINT ON PAPER:

1. Cover work surface with newspaper or plastic tablecloth.

2. Following manufacturer's directions, mix poster paint with water until it is the consistency of milk. Brush a thin layer onto tray. Run roller through paint. When using patterned roller, make sure motifs are well coated with paint. For mottled, fleecy effect, use the plain roller almost dry. Roll onto desired paper. One long steady roll gives best results. Run roller though paint again as necessary.

3. Let paint dry. Print back of paper, if desired.

4. Wash roller and paintbrush. Blot dry with paper towels. With marker, draw in sheep's features.

TO PRINT ON FABRIC:

1. Wash fabric to remove sizing. Press. Cover work surface with newspaper or plastic tablecloth.

2. Lay fabric flat on protected table surface. Tape down corners so fabric won't shift.

3. Mix fabric paint and spread a thin layer on tray. Run roller through paint and test print on a scrap of fabric. Print on fabric as you would on paper.

4. Let paint dry. To fix color, iron printed area according to manufacturer's directions.

THINGS TO MAKE FROM PRINTED PAPER

Gift Wrap

Print on plain newsprint or white shelf paper to create wonderful and inexpensive wrapping paper. Shelf paper is available at grocery stores and at office supply stores (often as tablecloth covering).

Gift Bow

YOU NEED

- **Roller-printed paper (on both sides)**
- **Needle and thread**

1. Cut a strip of printed paper, 24 x 1 in. (61.0 x 2.5 cm).

2. Bring end of strip up and over to form a loop approx 1 3/4 in. (4.5 cm) wide, or half the size of the finished bow. Make a second loop the same size opposite the first one. Folding back and forth, make another set of loops slightly smaller than the first, then make one small loop at center top (see Diagram). Cut off any excess. Tuck cut end under so it is well hidden. To hold bow together, stitch through center of loops. Knot thread ends at back of bow.

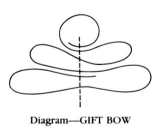

Diagram—GIFT BOW

Sheep Chain

YOU NEED

- **Strip of paper approx 4 3/4 in. (12.0 cm) wide x desired length of chain, roller-printed on both sides with small V motifs**
- **Felt-tip marker**
- **Tracing paper**

1. Trace large sheep (with legs) (page 59) onto tracing paper following adjustments indicated by broken line.

2. Accordion pleat strip of paper so each pleat measures 4 in. (10.0 cm) wide. Transfer outline of sheep onto top pleat so nose, chest and hind end are on folds. Cut out. Unfold chain.

3. With marker, draw in sheep's features.

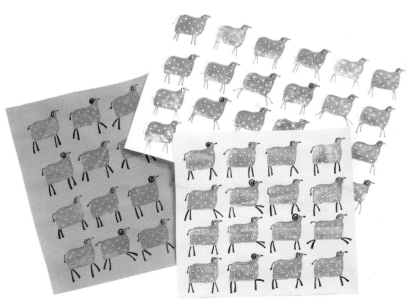

THINGS TO MAKE FROM PRINTED FABRIC

Lamb Ornament

1. Fold fabric in half so right sides are together and short edges meet. Trace around large sheep template (see Sheep Chain, Step 1) onto folded fabric. Cut out, leaving a 1/4 in. (0.6 cm) seam allowance on all edges.

2. Topstitch long edges of bias tape together. Cut four 1 5/8 in. (4.0 cm) lengths for legs, one 3 in. (7.5 cm) length for tail and one 2 in. (5.0 cm) length for ears.

3. With raw edges even, baste one end of legs to right side of one body piece as indicated on pattern. Knot one end of tail. Baste other end to body as for legs.

4. With right sides together, sew body pieces together using a 1/4 in. (0.6 cm) seam allowance and leaving open between legs. Clip curves. Turn right-side out. Press. Stuff firmly. Slipstitch opening closed.

5. With floss, embroider eyes, nose and mouth. Fold ear bias tape so raw ends meet at center point. Take a few stitches at center to secure. Having seam on underside, slipstitch ears across top of sheep's head.

6. Thread hanging loop of floss through top of sheep.

Ewe Pillow

To enlarge large sheep pattern, see General Directions (page 130).

1. Topstitch long edges of bias tape together. Cut four 4 1/2 in. (11.5 cm) lengths for legs, one 7 in. (18.0 cm) length for tail and two 3 1/2 in. (9.0 cm) lengths for ears.

2. Cut out and assemble as for Lamb Ornament (above).

3. Sew on beads for eyes. Embroider mouth and nose. Fold each piece of bias tape for ears in half so raw ends meet. Stitch ends together. Turn loops right-side out. Slipstitch in place on either side of head.

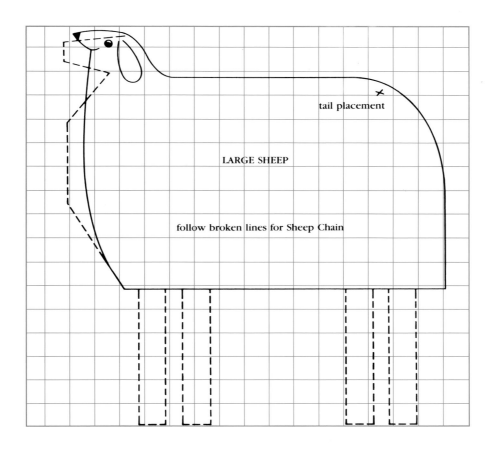

tail placement

LARGE SHEEP

follow broken lines for Sheep Chain

Child's Play Smock

(ages 4 to 7)

1. Press under 1/4 in. (0.6 cm), then 1 3/4 in. (4.5 cm), along one long edge of polyester/cotton fabric. Stitch close to first fold and then 5/8 in. (1.5 cm) from this to form casing.

2. Following measurements shown on Diagram, mark points A, B and C. Join these three points with a curved line. Cut along curved line for armhole. Cut two 8 1/2 in. (21.5 cm) lengths of wide bias tape. Bind upper and lower edges of armhole with this tape, turning under raw ends as you go. Reinforce stitching at ends. Repeat for opposite armhole.

3. Fuse interfacing to wrong side of printed fabric. Trace around large sheep template (see Sheep Chain, Step 1) onto fabric. Cut out. Pin sheep to front of smock where desired approx. 7 1/2 in. (19.0 cm) from bottom.

4. Topstitch long edges of narrow bias tape together. Cut five 1 5/8 in. (4.0 cm) lengths for legs and ear, and one 2 in. (5.0 cm) length for tail. Pin tail and legs in place, tucking raw ends under body. Fold ear bias tape in half so raw ends meet. Tuck raw ends under body where indicated for ear. Fold ear down toward face. Machine satin-stitch around sheep's body. With floss, embroider a French knot for eye.

For ram's horn, omit ear. Cut a 3 1/2 in. (9.0 cm) length of narrow bias tape. Roll end of each piece of bias tape for horn into a 1 in. (2.5 cm) diameter circle. With opposite end, roll a larger circle around the smaller one. Tack circles together with a few stitches and slipstitch in place behind eye.

5. Hem smock to desired length.

6. Topstitch long edge of remaining wide bias tape together. Thread through neck casing. Knot at both ends. Pull up and adjust gathers.

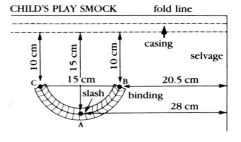

Cookie Cutter Christmas

DESIGNS BY MARY CORCORAN

Simple cookie cutter shapes are the starting point for delightful projects for children. Some of them can be made by children — with a little help from you. Cookie-Time Accessories, Paper Chains, Appliquéd Napkins, Stuffed Shapes and Cookie Cutter Dolls are all quick and easy gift ideas that can involve the whole family.

COOKIE-TIME ACCESSORIES

Trace around cookie cutters onto adhesive paper. Cut out shapes and stick onto a wooden basket, a paper gift bag or a clear acrylic cookie jar filled with cutout cookies, or onto clear plastic glasses or a plastic place mat.

APPLIQUÉD NAPKIN

Use a purchased cloth napkin or hem a 14 1/4 in. (approx. 36.0 cm) square of desired fabric. Iron light-weight fusible interfacing to back of scrap (approx. size of cookie cutter motif) of colored broadcloth. This gives broadcloth more body and makes appliquéing easier. Trace around cookie cutter onto back of interfaced scrap. Cut out. Position appliqué on corner of napkin. Machine satin-stitch in place around outline of shape. Decorate with ribbon bow, if appropriate.

PAPER CHAINS

Use colored tissue paper for lightweight chain to hang as a garland (it's easy to cut many layers at one time). For stiffer chain that stands up, use fewer layers of construction paper.

TO MAKE:

1. Cut paper into a long strip x height of cookie cutter. Trace around cookie cutter onto one end of strip so that

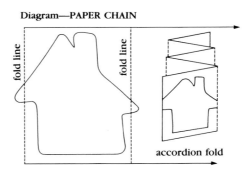

Diagram—PAPER CHAIN

fold line · fold line · accordion fold

outline of shape extends 1/4 in. (0.6 cm) beyond end of paper (see Diagram).

2. Accordion-fold strip so outline of shape extends 1/4 in. (0.6 cm) beyond folds at each side. Fold as many layers as you can comfortably cut at a time.

3. Cut along outline of shape. Open out chain. For long chain, make several strips and glue together.

STUFFED SHAPES

1. For small shapes, trace around cookie cutter onto interfaced fabric, and cut out two of each shape, leaving a 1/4 in. (0.6 cm) seam allowance. For pillow size, enlarge cookie cutter shape as follows:

Trace around cookie cutter onto paper. Draw a grid of horizontal and vertical lines 3/8 in. (1.0cm) apart on top of outline. Draw an enlarged grid on brown paper with lines approx 1 1/4 to 1 1/2 in. (3.0 to 4.0 cm) apart. Enlarge outline following General Directions (page 130). Pattern may also be enlarged photostatically, 300 to 400 percent. Cut out two enlarged shapes from interfaced fabric.

2. With right sides together, stitch shapes together using a 1/4 in. (0.6 cm) seam allowance and leaving a small opening along one edge. Clip corners and curves. Turn right-side out. Stuff with fiberfill. Slipstitch opening closed.

3. Thread hanging loop through top of small shapes for tree ornaments, or sew them in a row for a three-dimensional garland.

Cookie Cutter Dolls

YOU NEED

For each doll:
- **Piece of broadcloth, 24 x 18 in. (60.0 x 45.0 cm), for body**
- **Square of white broadcloth 4 in. (10.0 cm), for face**
- **Pieces of broadcloth in assorted colors, for clothes**
- **Piece of polyester fleece, 24 x 18 in. (60.0 x 45.1 cm)**
- **Lightweight fusible interfacing**
- **Matching threads**
- **Embroidery floss**
- **Two Velcro dot fasteners**
- **Geometry compass**
- **Water-soluble fabric marker**
- **Brown paper**
- **Tracing paper**

To enlarge doll patterns, see General Directions (page 130).

1. Cut two doll shapes from broadcloth and two from fleece.

2. Iron interfacing to back of white broadcloth square. With compass, draw a 3 1/2 in. (9.0 cm) circle on square (face). Using three strands of floss, embroider star eyes, mouth (running stitches) and cheeks (chain stitch in a circle). Cut out face. Pin to right side of head at a slight angle. Machine satin-stitch in place around edge.

3. Place doll front and back, right sides together, on top of two layers of fleece. Pin. Stitch all layers together using a 1/4 in. (0.6 cm) seam allowance, leaving a 2 in. (5.0 cm) opening along one side of body. Trim away excess fleece. Trim seam allowance. Clip corners and curves. Turn right-side out. Press. Stuff hands lightly. Topstitch finger lines. Stuff rest of body firmly. Slipstitch opening closed.

4. **Hair:** Cut 5/8 in. (1.5 cm) wide bias strips from broadcloth. Wrap strips around a 8 x 2 1/2 in. (20.0 x 6.0 cm) piece of paper, overlapping slightly. Zigzag lengthwise down center of paper. Tear away paper. Twist loops to look like curls. Stitch to top of doll's head.

5. **Girl's dress:** Trace dotted dress pattern lines onto tracing paper. Add 1/2 in. (1.3 cm) to all edges. Cut out paper pattern. From dress fabric, cut out one dress front. Fold pattern in half lengthwise (dress back pattern), and cut two backs from dress fabric, adding 3/4 in. (2.0 cm) to straight edges only.

With right sides together and using a 1/4 in. (0.6 cm) seam allowance, stitch front to backs at shoulders and sides. Press seams open. Turn under 1/4 in., then 1/4 in. again, down center back edges. Hem.

Cut a strip of broadcloth 45 x 3 1/8 in. (115.0 x 8.0 cm) for hem ruffle. Hem short ends. Fold in half so wrong sides are together and long edges meet. Press. Run a gathering thread down long raw edge, 1/4 in. (0.6 cm) from edge. Pull up thread. With right sides together, pin raw edge of ruffle to hem edge. Gather evenly. Stitch using a 1/4 in. seam allowance. Press ruffle down. Topstitch seam allowance 1/8 in. (0.3 cm) from seam.

Cut a strip of broadcloth 31 1/2 x 3 in. (80.0 x 8.0 cm) for neck ruffle. Hem short ends. Gather and stitch to neck edge as for hem ruffle. Sew Velcro fasteners to either side of back opening. Trace dotted pocket lines onto tracing paper. Add 1/2 in. (1.3 cm) to all edges.

Cut out paper pattern. Cut pocket from desired fabric. Iron interfacing to back of pocket. Turn under 1/2 in. on all edges.

Topstitch top edge. Topstitch remaining three edges in place on dress.

Cut two strips 9 1/2 x 1 1/8 in. (24.0 x 3.0 cm) for armhole binding. With right sides together, stitch one raw edge of binding around armhole. Cut off any excess length. Stitch ends together. Turn under 1/4 in. (0.6 cm) along remaining raw edge. Fold binding to inside and hem.

6. **Boy's overalls:** Trace dotted overall lines onto tracing paper. Add 1/2 in. (1.3 cm) to all edges. Cut out paper pattern. From overall fabric, cut two overall pieces. Turn under 1/4 in. (0.6 cm) at armholes, shoulders and neck.

Turn under 1/2 in. at leg hems. Satin-stitch over raw edges. With right sides together and using a 1/4 in. seam allowance, sew front to back at sides and inseam. Clip corners. Turn right-side out. Sew Velcro dot fasteners at shoulders.

Assemble and apply pocket to overalls as for dress. Cut a 4 in. (10.0 cm) square of broadcloth for hankie. Hem. Tuck into pocket.

For neckerchief pattern, draw a 11 in. (27.0 cm) square on paper. Cut out, then cut in half diagonally. Using this triangular pattern, cut one neckerchief from broadcloth. Hem. Tie around doll's neck.

Gifts for Little Hands to Make

DESIGNS BY SALLY MEDLAND

Nothing is more rewarding to a child than being able to say "... I made it myself!" With a bit of encouragement and an assortment of simple household materials, even little hands can produce presents such as a Tissue-Paper Tree, a Candy-Cane Reindeer and Mouse-in-a-Bed ornaments that family, friends and teachers will adore.

STRAWBERRY ORNAMENT

Paint a whole walnut with shiny red paint. When paint dries, dab on dots of glue with toothpick and glue tiny white seed beads in place. Glue a loop of gold thread to top of strawberry. Cut out green leaves from scraps of felt. Glue leaves to top of strawberry.

CANDY-CANE REINDEER

Twist a long colored pipe cleaner around top of candy cane. Bend ends into shape of funny antlers. Glue on a little red pom-pom nose and two rolly eyes. Tie fancy bow around neck.

TISSUE-PAPER SNOWMAN AND TREE

Cut out a Christmas shape, such as a Christmas tree, a snowman or a wreath, from cardboard. Cut colored tissue paper into many 2 in. (approx. 5.0 cm) squares. Fold each square over pointer finger and scrunch together at fingertip. Glue to cardboard so shape is completely covered. Decorate tree with little red tissue-paper balls or pom-poms for berries, or white balls for snowflakes. Decorate snowman with pipe cleaner or paper bow and paper hat. Trim wreath with paper bow and berries.

MOUSE-IN-A-BED ORNAMENT

With a marker, draw a mouse face on a hazelnut. Cut mouse ears from colored felt and glue them to each side of hazelnut head. Glue a loop of thread inside a half-walnut shell. Glue a piece of elastic band at pointed end of walnut shell for mouse tail. Glue hazelnut head to other end of walnut shell. Dab glue around inside edge of walnut. Poke a little piece of fabric into shell to cover up mouse. Hang on tree with loop of thread.

REINDEER GIFT TAG

Cut a small diamond from construction paper. Fold in half to make a triangle. Cut two holly-shaped antlers from green paper and glue to top of triangle head along fold. Draw two eyes with marker, and glue on a tiny red pom-pom nose.

DUCK ORNAMENT

Gather together little scraps of wood or wood bits from a craft store, or cut pieces of cardboard into different shapes. Paint with bright Christmassy-colored acrylic paint. Place on waxed paper to dry. Glue together into shape of duck. Decorate with ribbon. Glue wire Christmas tree hanger to back.

CHAPTER 4

Heirloom Treasures

Treetop Angel

DESIGN BY CAROL SCHMIDT

Create an exquisite angel to adorn the top of your tree for years to come. Golden threads highlight the moiré taffeta, an antique lace doily with crocheted edgings forms the wings and the delicate face is embroidered with floss. A work of art this special is sure to become a family heirloom.

YOU NEED

- **Piece of white moiré taffeta, 12 x 8 1/2 in. (30.0 x 21.0 cm)**
- **Piece of white felt, 12 x 8 1/2 in. (30.0 x 21.0 cm)**
- **Scrap of flesh-tone felt**
- **White crocheted doily with fluted edge, approx. 6 3/4 in. (17.0 cm) in diameter**
- **Silk or viscose embroidery floss, peach and dark coral**
- **DMC embroidery floss:**

  No. 931 — gray-blue

  No. 732 — olive

  No. 938 — dark brown

  No. 498 — red

- **DMC Fil Or (gold)**
- **Gold lamé yarn**
- **No. 10 white crochet cotton**
- **No. 8 white DMC Coton Perlé**
- **White and flesh-tone sewing thread**
- **Embroidery hoop, approx. 12 in. (30.0 cm) in diameter**
- **Muslin to fit hoop**
- **Embroidery needle**
- **U.S. size B (2.00 mm) and U.S. size D (3.00 mm) crochet hooks**
- **Small artist's paint brush**
- **Powder blush**

For crochet abbreviations and to enlarge angel pattern, see General Directions (page 130). Refer to Embroidery Diagram for embroidery stitches.

1. Cut two angel shapes from taffeta, for front and back, and two from felt, for liner. Cut face and hands from flesh-tone felt.

2. Stretch muslin in hoop. Baste one taffeta piece (front of angel) to muslin.

3. Sew felt face to front, using tiny backstitches. With a single strand of floss and small outline stitches, embroider brown eyes and red mouth. Fill in mouth with small straight stitches.

4. With Fil Or, work spaced blanket stitches around edge of face, varying the length of the stitches to shape halo. Starting at edge of face with same thread, weave over and under blanket stitches, going through fabric only at each end of halo. Continue weaving back and forth around face, packing weaving solid until halo is filled. With same thread, embroider three-petal flowers around edge of halo using detached chain stitch.

5. With three strands of peach floss, embroider French knots, closely spaced around edge of face, wrapping floss three times around needle for each knot.

6. With Fil Or, stem-stitch inner and outer lines of dress. Chain-stitch bottom line of yoke.

7. With a single strand of dark coral floss, fill yoke with laid thread work. Following Laid Thread Diagram, tack down laid threads with crosses (using single strand of gray-blue floss) and French knots (using four strands of olive floss).

8. With Fil Or, embroider center panel as shown.

9. Working from inside to outside edge with Fil Or, fill in side panels of dress between stem-stitch outlines with the following row sequence: 1 row chain stitch, 1 row slanted feather stitch, 1 row chain stitch, *3 rows closely spaced stem stitch, 1 row chain stitch. Repeat from * until area is completely filled.

10. Sew on felt hands using tiny backstitches.

11. Remove muslin/taffeta from hoop. With right sides of taffeta together, stitch front to back using a 1/4 in. (0.6 cm) seam allowance, leaving bottom edge open. Turn right-side out.

12. Stitch felt liner pieces together using a 3/8 in. (1.0 cm) seam allowance, leaving bottom edge open. Trim seam allowance close to stitching. With wrong sides together, fit liner inside taffeta angel. Turn under 1/4 in. (0.6 cm) around bottom edge on both fabrics. With Coton Perlé, buttonhole-stitch the edges together, making stitches 1/8 in. (0.3 cm) apart.

13. **Lower hem fringe:** With smaller crochet hook and crochet cotton, work in rounds as follows:
Rnd 1: Work 2 dc in each blanket stitch along bottom edge, join to first dec with sl st.
Rnd 2: *Sk 1 st, 5 dc in next st (this forms shell). Rep from * to end of rnd.
Rnd 3: Sl st in first 3 sts of first shell, ch 5, *1 sc in

third dc of next shell, ch 5 (this forms bar). Rep from * to end of rnd, sl st in third sl st at beg of rnd to join.
Rnd 4: Sl st in first 2 sts of bar, 1 sc around same bar, 5 dc in sc, *1 sc around next bar, 5 dc in next sc. Rep from * to end of rnd.
Rnd 5: As Rnd 3.
Rnd 6: Sl st in first 2 sts of bar, 1 sc around same bar, ch 5, *1 sc around next bar, ch 5. Rep from * to end of rnd and join to first sc with sl st.
Rnd 7: Work 7 dc into each bar of previous rnd, join to first dc with sl st.
Rnd 8: As Rnd 2. Fasten off and weave in yarn end.

14. **Upper hem fringe:** With smaller crochet hook and gold lamé yarn, work upper fringe on top of lower fringe as follows:
Rnd 1: Work 2 sc in each blanket stitch along bottom edge, working one on each side of 2 dc that were worked in first rnd of crochet cotton fringe. Join to first sc with sl st.
Rods 2 to 4: Work as given for lower hem fringe, working 4 dc instead of 5 dc in sc in Rnd. 4.

15. **Wings:** Fold doily in half. With larger crochet hook and gold lamé yarn, sc along curved edge through both layers of doily, being careful to keep work flat. Ch 3, turn.
Row 2: Dc to end of row, turn.
Row 3: *Sk 1 st, work 5 dc in next st. Rep from * to end of row. Fasten off and weave in yarn end.
With straight edge at top, tack wings to back of angel at center point and at side edges.

16. Using paintbrush, highlight cheeks with a little blush.

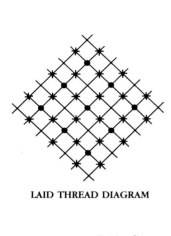

LAID THREAD DIAGRAM

——————	Cutting line (body, face, hands)
⊔⊔⊔	Blanket stitch
∿∿∿	Stem stitch
∞∞∞	Chain stitch
———	Straight stitch
⊶	Detached chain stitch
●	French knot

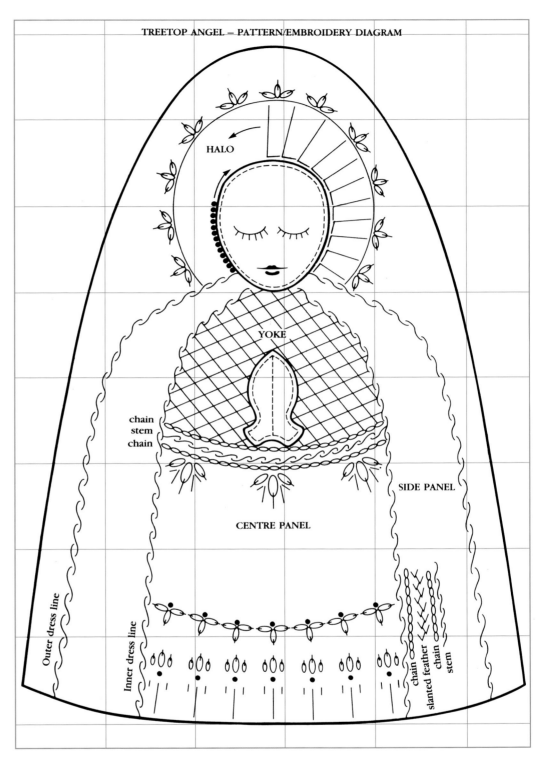

TREETOP ANGEL – PATTERN/EMBROIDERY DIAGRAM

HALO

YOKE

chain
stem
chain

SIDE PANEL

CENTRE PANEL

Outer dress line

Inner dress line

chain
slanted feather
chain
stem

Santa and Mrs. Claus

DESIGN BY MARGARET STEPHENSON COOLE

Christmas just wouldn't be complete without a visit from jolly Santa and Mrs. Claus. Here is the most adorable little pair imaginable. Let them preside over your holiday festivities and bring the happy spirit of Christmas into your home.

YOU NEED

For both dolls:

- 5/8 yd. (0.50 m) flesh-tone broadcloth, 45 in. (approx. 115.0 cm) wide
- 1/4 yd. (0.20 m) red-and-white-striped cotton, 45 in. (115.0 cm) wide
- Matching threads
- Buttonhole twist thread, flesh-tone and navy blue
- 0.20 m red embroidery floss
- Four navy-blue buttons, approx. 1/4 in. (0.7 cm) in diameter
- Four clear beads, approx. 3/8 in. (0.4 cm) in diameter
- Small amount of white washed sheep's fleece (available at weaving supply stores)
- Doll-making needle
- Embroidery needle
- Pink colored pencil
- Polyester fiberfill
- Spray starch

- Brown paper

For both dolls' clothes:

- 3/4 yd. (0.60 m) red velveteen, 45 in. (approx. 115.0 cm) wide
- 1/2 yd. (0.40 m) red broadcloth, 45 in. (115.0 cm) wide
- 1/4 yd. (0.20 m) polka-dot cotton fabric, 45 in. (115.0 cm) wide
- 1/4 yd. (0.20 m) white woven-stripe cotton fabric, 45 in. (115.0 cm) wide
- 3/8 yd. (0.30 m) white woven-check cotton fabric, 45 in. (115.0 cm) wide
- 1/4 yd. red-and-white-striped knit fabric, 60 in. (approx. 150.0 cm) wide
- Piece of white short-pile fake fur, 14 x 4 3/4 in. (35.0 x 12.0 cm)

- Piece of black felt, 12 in. (30.0 cm) square
- Scrap of red felt
- 3/4 yd. (0.70 m) white pre-gathered lace, approx. 1 5/8 in. (4.0 cm) wide
- 1/2 yd. (0.40 m) white pregathered lace, approx. 3/4 in. (2.0 cm) wide
- 1/2 yd. (0.50 m) white pre-gathered lace, approx. 3/8 in. (1.0 cm) wide
- 3/4 yd. (0.70 m) white flat lace, 3/8 in. (1.0 cm) wide
- 1/4 yd. (0.20 m) red satin ribbon, 1/8 in. (0.3 cm) wide
- 3/8 yd. (0.30 m) black velvet ribbon, 1/4 in. (0.6 cm) wide
- 3/8 yd. (0.30 m) black braided piping, approx. 5/8 in. (1.5 cm) wide

- 1 1/8 yd. (1.00 m) narrow red cord
- 1/2 yd. (0.40 m) black twill tape, 3/8 in. (1.0 cm) wide
- 5/8 yd. (0.60 m) white elastic, 1/4 in. (0.6 cm) wide
- 3/8 yd. (0.30 m) white elastic, 1/8 in. (0.3 cm) wide
- 1/4 yd. (0.20 m) black elastic, 1/4 in. (0.6 cm) wide
- Two black beads, approx. 3/16 in. (0.4 cm) in diameter
- Eight red beads, approx. 3/16 in. (0.4 cm) in diameter
- Four red buttons, 3/8 in. (1.0 cm) in diameter
- Ten black snap fasteners, approx. 3/16 in. (0.5 cm) in diameter
- Four jingle bells
- Geometry compass

The finished dolls are approx. 12 in. (30.0 cm) tall.

TO MAKE:

Note: Cut velveteen so direction of nap runs from top to bottom of each piece. Use closely spaced machine stitches and a 1/4 in. (0.6 cm) seam allowance throughout, unless otherwise indicated. Backstitch at the beginning and end of all seams.

To enlarge patterns for dolls and clothes, see General Directions (page 130).

DOLLS

1. **For Santa:** From flesh-tone broadcloth, cut body fronts, body backs, arms and legs.

For Mrs. Claus: From flesh-tone broadcloth, cut arms, then following broken pattern lines, cut body fronts and backs. From striped cotton, cut legs.

2. **Legs:** With right sides together, stitch two leg pieces together, leaving open at top. Clip curves. Turn right-side out. Stuff to dotted line (knee). Fold leg so front and back seams align. Topstitch across knee line. Stuff upper leg lightly and machine-stitch closed 1/4 in. (0.6 cm) from raw edge. Repeat for other leg.

3. **Body:** With right sides together, stitch two body front pieces down center front seam and two body back pieces down center back seam. Clip curves. With right sides together and toes pointing toward tummy, stitch legs to bottom edge of body front. With right sides together, stitch body front to body back, leaving bottom edge open between dots. Clip curves. Turn right-side out. Stuff head, maintaining shape of nose and chin. Stuff body firmly. Turn under 1/4 in. (0.6 cm) around bottom edge. Slipstitch opening closed.

4. **Arms:** With right sides together, stitch two arm pieces together, leaving open between dots. Clip curves. Turn right-side out. Stuff firmly. Turn under 1/4 in. (0.6 cm) around opening. Slipstitch closed. Topstitch finger lines on hand. Repeat for other arm.

Thread doll-making needle with flesh-tone buttonhole thread. Stitching through shoulder circles, push needle through one arm, through body and out through other arm several times. Thread a clear bead onto last stitch on outside of each arm. Knot thread securely. To allow

arm movement, wind buttonhole thread around threads between each arm and shoulder, forming a short shank.

5. **Face:** Mark placement of eyes with pins. Thread doll-making needle with flesh-tone buttonhole thread. Push needle in at top of head and out at one eye. Push

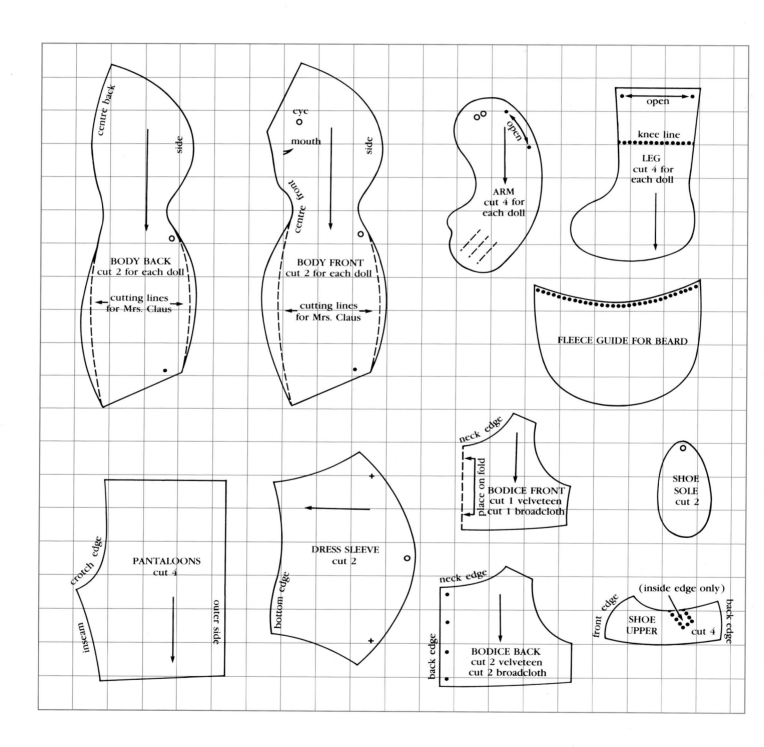

needle back into same eye, taking a 1/8 in. (0.3 cm) stitch, and out at other eye. Shape bridge of nose by pinching nose firmly while stitching several times through face from eye to eye, pulling thread tightly. Push needle out at top of head. Knot thread securely.

Thread needle with blue buttonhole thread. Push needle in at back of head, out at one eye and through blue button. Push needle back through button and out at back of head, pulling button tightly toward back of head. Repeat three or four times. Repeat for other eye.

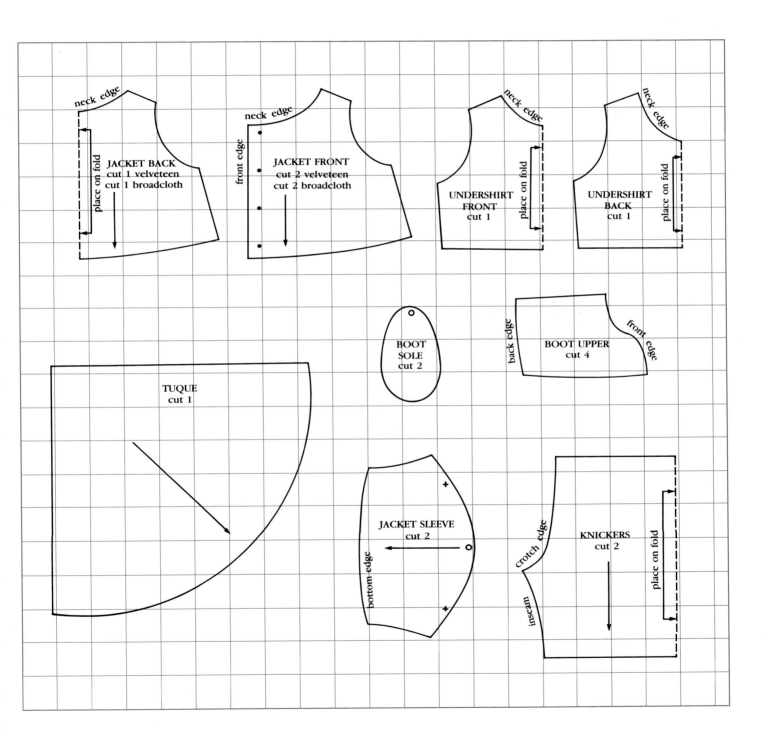

With a single strand of floss and outline stitch, embroider mouth. Color cheeks lightly with colored pencil.

6. **Hair:** Shape a handful of fleece into a circle approx. 6 in. (15.0 cm) in diameter and 2 in. (5.0 cm) thick, having long fibers running in same direction. Supporting fleece with both hands, gently dip several times into lukewarm water. Set fleece on a towel and blow-dry with hair dryer on low setting. As it dries, mold and fluff fleece into shape to fit doll's head. When dry, pin to head so fibers run from side to side. Arrange curls and wisps to frame face and trim off any excess. Tack hair to top of head and around hairline using tiny stitches 3/4 in. (2.0 cm) apart. Stitch a line of closely spaced stitches down center of head for part. Spray lightly with starch.

7. **Beard and moustache (Santa only):**
Prepare fleece as for hair. As it dries, mold and fluff it into the beard shape shown on pattern, having fibers running lengthwise. Along face edge indicated by dotted line, wrap some fibers to underside to give a smooth edge. Tack to chin and cheeks. Fluff out and trim. Spray lightly with starch.

Form moustache from fleece. Pinch in at center and tack securely in place under nose. Spray lightly with starch.

CLOTHES — MRS. CLAUS

1. **Shoes:** From black felt, cut shoe uppers, shoe soles and two straps, 3 1/8 x 1/4 in. (8.0 cm x 0.6 cm). Edgestitch along two long edges and one short end of each strap. Stitch front edge of two shoe uppers together using a 1/8 in. (0.3 cm) seam allowance. On one side only, pin unstitched end of strap to inside edge of upper where indicated by dotted line. Edgestitch around top edge of upper, catching strap in stitching. With right sides together and using a 1/8 in. seam allowance, stitch back seam then stitch sole to bottom edge of upper (match circle to center front seam). Turn right-side out. Repeat for other shoe, attaching strap to opposite side so you will have a right and a left shoe.
Slip shoes on doll, having straps at inside of each foot. Cross straps over feet and secure to outside of each shoe with a few hand stitches. Thread a black bead onto last stitch and knot thread securely.

2. **Pantaloons:** Cut pantaloons from polka-dot fabric. With right sides together, stitch two pieces together down side seam. Press seam open. Turn under 1/8 in. (0.3 cm) then 1/4 in. (0.6 cm) along bottom edge. Topstitch. Stitch 3/4 in. (2.0 cm) wide gathered lace along hemmed edge. With right sides together, stitch inseam. Repeat with remaining two pantaloon pieces. Turn one leg right-side out and insert into other leg so right sides are together and inseams are aligned. Stitch crotch seam. Turn pantaloons right-side out. Run 2 rows of gathering stitches around top edge. Cut a 10 1/4 in. (26.0 cm) length of 1/4 in. (0.6 cm) white elastic. Overlap and stitch ends together. Pin elastic around top edge of pantaloons, adjusting gathers to fit. Machine-zigzag in place. Remove gathering threads.

3. **Petticoat:** From white woven-stripe fabric, cut a 26 x 4 3/4 in. (66.0 x 12.0 cm) rectangle. Fold in half so right sides are together and short edges meet. Stitch short edges together. Press seam open.

Turn under 1/8 in. (0.3 cm) then 1/4 in. (0.6 cm) around one raw edge. Topstitch. Stitch right side of 1 5/8 in. (4.0 cm) gathered lace to wrong side of hemmed edge. Gather top edge and attach elastic as for pantaloons.

4. **Dress:** From velveteen, cut bodice front, bodice backs, sleeves and a 26 x 8 in. (66.0 x 20.0 cm) rectangle for skirt. From broadcloth, cut bodice front, bodice backs (facings) and two bias strips, 5 1/2 x 1 3/8 in. (14.0 x 3.5 cm) for sleeve facings. With right sides together, stitch bodice front to bodice backs at shoulders. Press seams open. Repeat with bodice facings. With right sides of bodice and facing together, stitch down back and around neck edges. Clip curves. Turn right-side out. Press. Baste bodice to facing around armholes, waist and side edges.

With right sides together, stitch one long edge of sleeve facing along cuff edge of sleeve. Gather top edge of sleeve between Xs. With right sides together, pin sleeve to armhole, matching circle to shoulder seam and adjusting gathers evenly. Stitch. Remove gathering threads. Trim seam allowance to 1/8 in. (0.3 cm) and zigzag along raw edges. Repeat for other sleeve. With right sides together, stitch sleeve and side seams. Turn under 1/4 in. (0.6 cm) on raw edge of sleeve facings. Fold facings under along seam line and slipstitch to wrong side.

Gather one long edge of skirt. Press under 1/2 in.

(1.3 cm) on each short edge. With right sides together, pin gathered edge of skirt to bodice, aligning folds at each end with back edges of bodice and adjusting gathers evenly in between. Stitch. Open out folded edges of skirt. With right sides together and using a 1/2 in. seam allowance, stitch center back seam to within 2 3/4 in. (7.0 cm) of bodice seam. Press seam open. Machine-zigzag raw edges of seam allowance.

Machine-zigzag along bottom edge of skirt. Turn under 2 in. (5.0 cm) and hem. Slipstitch 3/8 in. (1.0 cm) flat lace over raw edge of hem. Slipstitch 3/8 in. (1.0 cm) gathered lace around inside edge of neck and cuffs. Sew four snap fasteners to bodice back. On outside of bodice, sew a red bead over each snap.

5. **Apron:** From white woven-check fabric, cut a 12 x 7 1/2 in. (30.0 x 19.0 cm) rectangle for apron, two 3 1/2 in. (9.0 cm) squares for pocket and a 36 1/2 x 2 in. (93.0 x 5.0 cm) strip for tie. Turn under 1/8 in. (0.3 cm) then 1/4 in. (0.6 cm) along short edges of apron. Topstitch. Turn under 1/4 in., then 1 5/8 in. (4.0 cm), along one long edge. Topstitch. Press under 1/4 in. along one edge of each pocket square. With right sides together and folded edges matching, stitch two pocket squares together along three raw edges. Clip corners. Turn right-side out. Having

open edge at bottom, topstitch pocket to apron front. Place pin at center of long raw edge of apron. Gather this edge. Pull up gathering thread so gathered edge measures 5 in. (13.0 cm) long. Knot threads. Place pin at center of one long edge of tie. With right sides together and center pins matching, baste apron to tie, adjusting gathers evenly. Fold tie in half so right sides are together and long edges meet. Stitch along unbasted section of long edges and up short ends.

Clip corners. Turn right-side out. Press. Turn under 1/4 in. along center of tie at back of apron. Topstitch opening closed.

6. **Dust cap:** From white woven-check fabric, cut a 16 1/2 x 7 in. (42.0 x 18.0 cm) rectangle. Fold in half so right sides are together and short edges meet. Stitch short edges together leaving 1/4 in. (0.6 cm) openings 3/8 in. (1.0 cm) from one raw edge (top) and 1/4 in. from opposite raw edge (bottom). Press seam open. To make top casing, turn under 3/8 in. around top edge and topstitch 1/4 in. from fold. To make bottom casing, turn under 1 5/8 in. (approx. 4.0 cm) around bottom edge and topstitch first 1 in. (2.5 cm), then 1 3/8 in. (3.5 cm), from fold. Turn right-side out. Cut a 8 in. (20.0 cm) length of red ribbon and thread through

top casing. Draw up and tie tightly in a bow. Tack bow in place. Cut a 10 1/4 in. (26.0 cm) length of white 1/8 in. (0.3 cm) elastic and thread through bottom casing. Overlap and stitch ends together.

CLOTHES — SANTA

1. **Boots:** From black felt, cut boot uppers and boot soles. Stitch front edge of two boot uppers together using a 1/8 in. (0.3 cm) seam allowance. Stitch piping around inside top edge so rolled edge extends beyond felt. Stitch black velvet ribbon around outside top edge. With right sides together and using a 1/8 in. seam allowance, stitch back seam and then stitch sole to bottom edge of upper (match circle to center front seam). Turn right-side out. Repeat for other boot.

2. **Undershirt:** From striped knit fabric, cut undershirt front and back. With right sides together, stitch front to

back at shoulders and sides. Turn under 1/4 in. (0.6 cm) on all raw edges. Machine-zigzag or stretch-stitch in place.

3. **Knickers:** From red velveteen, cut knickers. From red broadcloth, cut a strip 14 1/4 x 1 3/8 in. (36.0 x 3.5 cm) for waistband facing. Fold each knicker leg in half along fold line so right sides are together. Stitch inseam. Press seam open. Machine-zigzag around bottom edge. Run two lines of gathering stitches around bottom edge. Cut a 4 in. (10.0 cm) length of 1/4 in. (0.6 cm) elastic. Overlap and stitch ends together. Pin elastic around inside bottom edge, adjusting gathers evenly. Machine-zigzag in place. Remove gathering threads. Repeat for other leg.

Turn one leg right-side out and insert into other leg so right sides are together and inseams are aligned. Stitch crotch seam. Turn knickers right-side out. Fold waistband facing in half so right sides are together and short ends meet. Stitch short ends together. With right sides together, stitch one edge of facing around waist of knickers. Turn under 1/4 in. (0.6 cm) or remaining raw edge. Fold facing to inside along seam. Slipstitch in place. Slip knickers on doll.

4. **Suspenders:** Cut two 8 in. (20.0 cm) lengths of twill tape. Pin one end of each to back waist of knickers, 3/8 in. (1.0 cm) to either side of seam. Cross tapes, bring over shoulders and pin ends to front waist, 3/4 in. (2.0 cm) to either side of seam. Stitch red buttons to back of knickers over tape ends. Tack tapes together at crossover, and sew on a small diamond of red felt. At front, stitch snap fasteners to tape ends and to waist. Stitch red buttons to outside of suspenders over each snap fastener.

5. **Jacket:** From velveteen, cut jacket back, fronts and sleeves. From broadcloth, cut jacket back and fronts (facings). With right sides together, stitch jacket fronts to back at shoulders. Press seams open. Repeat with facings. With right sides of jacket and facing together, stitch down front and around neck edges. Clip curves. Turn right-side out. Press. Baste jacket to facing around armholes, bottom and side edges. From fake fur, cut two strips 4 3/4 x 1 3/8 in. (12.0 x 3.5 cm) for cuff trim and one strip 6 1/2 x 1 5/8 in. (42.0 x 4.0 cm) for hem trim. From broadcloth, cut the same on the bias, for trim facings.

With right sides together, stitch one long edge of cuff facing to cuff trim. Finger-press seam allowance toward trim and secure with tiny catch stitches. With right sides together, stitch opposite long edge of cuff trim to cuff edge of sleeve. Finger-press as before. Gather top edge of sleeve between Xs. With right sides together, pin sleeve to armhole, matching circle to shoulder seam and adjusting gathers evenly. Stitch. Remove gathering threads. Trim seam allowance to 1/8 in. (0.3 cm) and zigzag along raw edges. Repeat for other sleeve. With right sides together, stitch sleeve and side seams. Turn under 1/4 in. (0.6 cm) on raw edge of cuff facings.

Fold facings under along seam line and slipstitch to wrong side. Stitch hem trim and facing together and sew to bottom edge of jacket as for cuff trim. Turn under 1/4 in. on raw edge of facing. Fold along seam line so right side of trim and facing are together. Stitch ends in line with front edges of jacket. Clip corners. Turn right-side out. Slipstitch facing to wrong side. Sew four snap fasteners down front of jacket. On outside, sew a red bead over each snap.

6. From velveteen, cut hat. From fake fur, cut a strip 14 x 1 3/8 in. (35.0 x 3.5 cm) for trim and a 1 3/8 in. diameter circle for pom-pom. From broadcloth, cut a bias strip 14 x 1 3/8 in., for trim facing. Stitch trim and facing together and sew to curved edge of hat as for cuff trim. Fold so right sides are together and straight edges meet. Stitch straight edges together. Turn under 1/4 in. (0.6 cm) on raw edge of facing. Fold facing under along seam line and slipstitch to wrong side. Run a line of gathering stitches around edge of fur circle. Place a small amount of fiberfill on wrong side. Pull up gathering thread to form a ball. Knot thread. Slipstitch closed. Sew pom-pom to tip of hat.

7. **Sack:** From velveteen, cut a 12 1/2 x 8 in. (32.0 x 20.0 cm) rectangle and a 3 1/2 in. (9.0 cm) diameter circle. Fold rectangle in half so right sides are together and short edges meet. Stitch short edges together, leaving a 3/8 in. (1.0 cm) opening 2 3/4 in. (7.0 cm) from one corner (top edge). Machine-zigzag around top edge. Turn under 1 5/8 in. (4.0 cm). To make casing, topstitch 1 3/8 in. (3.5 cm), then 1 in. (2.5 cm) from fold. Run two lines of gathering stitches around bottom edge. With right sides together, pin gathered edge around circle, adjusting gathers evenly. Stitch. Remove gathering threads. Machine-zigzag raw edge. Turn right-side out.

Cut red cord in half. Thread both lengths through casing. Tie a bell to end of each cord.

Homespun Nativity

DESIGN BY MARY CORCORAN

This simple crèche scene, symbolic of the first Christmas, expresses the true spirit of the season. The figures are dressed in homespun fabrics, and assorted trims are added for an effect that is both natural and artistic. It's a heartwarming scene destined to become the focal point of your Christmas celebrations.

YOU NEED

For 8 figures:

- 1/2 yd. (0.40 m) linen fabric, 45 in. (approx. 115.0 cm) wide
- Eight pieces of coordinating linen fabric, each 7 in. (18.0 cm) square, for cloaks
- 1 1/2 yd. (1.40 m) ecru lace or ribbon, 3/8 in. (1.0 cm) wide
- Assorted scraps of lace trim
- Matching threads
- Polyester fiberflll
- Piece of cardboard, 8 in. (20.5 cm) square
- Two wooden beads, 1 in. (2.5 cm) in diameter

- Small beads or pebbles
- Large wooden bead and small piece of cork to fit hole in bead
- Three twigs, approx. 7 in. (18.0 cm) long
- White craft glue
- Gesso
- Stiff-bristle artist's paintbrush
- Red and black permanent fine-tip felt markers
- Geometry compass
- Brown paper

Note: Use a 1/4 in. (0.6 cm) seam allowance throughout.

To enlarge body pattern, see General Directions (page 130).

1. From large length of linen, cut eight bodies, eight 5 x 1 5/8 in. (12.5 x 4.0 cm) rectangles for arms, eight 3 3/8 in. (8.5 cm) diameter base circles and three 2 1/2 x 2 in. (6.5 x 5.0 cm) rectangles, one for baby body, one for diaper and one for lamb.

From cardboard, cut eight 2 1/8 in. (5.5 cm) diameter base circles and one face shape to be used as a pattern only.

2. **Face:** Fold each body in half lengthwise so wrong sides are together. Having fold on left side for four figures and on the right side for remaining four figures, center and trace around face pattern 3/4 in. (2.0 cm) below top edge of body. Paint face with gesso. Let dry. Apply two more coats. With markers, practice drawing facial features on scrap paper. Select the ones you like best and draw them on the fabric faces.

3. **Hair and beard:** Unravel threads from leftover fabric. For straight hair and beard, wrap strands of thread around hairline and under chin. Tack in place. For curly hair, loop five strands of thread as shown in Diagrams 1 and 2, and tack to head and around face. For Mary, gather together several strands of thread and tie in the middle. Tack to center and down sides of head.

4. **Body:** Fold each body so right sides are together. Stitch side seam. With doubled thread, run a line of gathering stitches around top edge. Pull up thread and knot securely. Turn body right-side out. Stuff. Turn under 1/4 in. (0.6 cm) around bottom edge.

5. **Base:** Run a line of gathering stitches around edge of each fabric base. Place cardboard base inside fabric circle. Pull up thread and gather evenly around cardboard. Knot securely. Slipstitch base to bottom of body.

6. **Arms:** Fold each arm piece in half so right sides are together and long edges meet. Stitch long raw edge and both ends. Cut in half so you have two narrow tubes. Clip corners. Turn both tubes right-side out. Stuff each arm lightly. Hand-stitch finger lines at closed end, pulling gently on stitches to make hand curve slightly. Slipstitch open end of arms to each side of body.

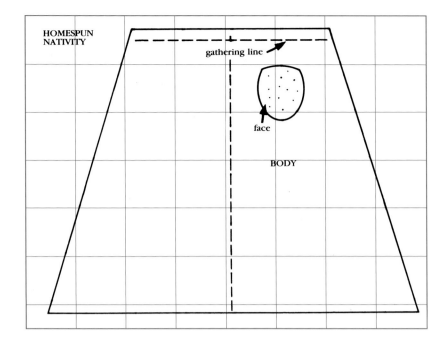

HOMESPUN NATIVITY

gathering line

face

BODY

Diagram 1 **Diagram 2**

1/4 in. (0.6 cm) around open end. Slipstitch closed. Paint a small face on one end of body with three coats of gesso. Let dry. Draw features. Slipstitch lace trim around length of baby's body. Slipstitch baby in Mary's arms.

9. **Diaper:** Topstitch around diaper, 1/4 in. (0.6 cm) from edge. Fray edges. Fold in half and slipstitch in Joseph's hands.

10. **Lamb:** Fold lamb fabric in half so right sides are together and long edges meet. Stitch long edge and one end, curving stitching at end to form lamb's head. Trim. Turn right-side out. Stuff. Turn under 1/4 in. (0.6 cm) around open end. Slipstitch closed. Paint both sides of one end of body (head) with gesso. Let dry. Draw eyes and nose. With three strands of unraveled linen, make loops for ears and fleece. Tack in place. Slipstitch lamb in shepherd's arms.

11. Slipstitch twigs in hands of each shepherd.

12. Glue small beads or pebbles onto wooden buttons to represent frankincense and myrrh. Glue cork into hole in large beads to represent a vessel of gold. Glue gifts in hands of wise men.

7. **Cloak:** Topstitch along one edge (bottom) of each cloak square, 1/4 in. (0.6 cm) from edge. Fray edge. Topstitch lace along bottom edge just above fringe. Turn under 1/4 in. on remaining raw edges. Topstitch. Center top of cloak over head. Pin top corners underneath arms about 1 in. (2.5 cm) below face. Pin bottom corners in place, in line with top corners. Smooth fabric from hem up to arms. Pin just below arms, making a small fold to form sleeves. Tack edges of sleeves to body. Remove pins. Slipstitch lace trim around heads of wise men.

8. **Baby:** Fold baby fabric in half so right sides are together and long edges meet. Stitch long edge. Run a line of gathering stitches around one end. Pull up thread and knot securely. Turn right-side out. Stuff. Turn under

CHAPTER 5

Crafts for Bazaars

Bazaar Bests

Nothing makes a bazaar a success more than high-quality, handmade articles. Here are thirteen irresistible ideas that are definite super sellers for any Christmas bazaar or sale. Choose from such great items as tiny Pinecone Teddies and adorable Pipe-Cleaner Clowns. Most are easy to make in quantity and easy on the budget, too. Included in the collection is a whimsical reindeer — make him your mascot, or offer him as a prize in a money-making raffle.

Snowflake Ski Bands and Mitts

To fit an average-sized woman's head and hand size.

YOU NEED

- Two balls (50 g) Patons Canadiana yarn, MC
- One ball (40 g) Patons Valencia yarn, CC
- One ball (50 g) Patons Cotton Sahara yarn, A
- One pair U.S. size 6 (4.00 mm) needles
- U.S. size 6 (4.00 mm) circular needle, 16 in. (40.0 cm) long OR whichever needles you require to produce the tension given below
- U.S. size F (4.00 mm) crochet hook

TENSION:

21 sts and 28 rows = 4 ins (10 cm) in St st. Work to the exact tension with the specified yarn to obtain satisfactory results.

TO SAVE TIME, TAKE TIME TO CHECK TENSION.

Note: The contrasting colored motifs are worked by carrying yarn not in use loosely across back of work, but never over more than 3 sts. When it must pass over more than 3 sts, weave it over and under color in use on next st or at center of sts it passes over. When changing colors, in order to prevent a hole, pass color to be used under and around to right of color just used.

See General Directions (page 130) for knitting abbreviations.

HEADBAND

With MC and circular needle, cast on 100 sts. Join in a round and place a marker on the first st.

Work in St st (k every round), following ski band graph (rep 20 sts of graph 5 times across round) to end of graph.

Next rnd: Purl

Next rnd: Knit. Break MC and CC. Join A and work in St st until work in A measures 1/4 in. (0.6 cm) less than work in MC and CC. Break A.

Next rnd: Join MC and knit.

Cast off loosely.

TO FINISH:

Fold headband in half so wrong sides are together. With MC, loosely slipstitch cast-on edge to cast-off edge.

MITTS

Right mitt:

**With MC and straight needles, cast on 40 sts. Work 22 rows in (k1 tbl, p1) ribbing, ending with right side facing for next row.

To make thumb gusset:

Beg with a k row, work 8 rows in St st.**

Row 9: K21, inc 1 st in each of next 2 sts, k to end of row.

Rows 10, 12, 14 and 16: Purl.

Row 11: K21, inc 1 st in next st, k2, inc 1 st in next st, k to end of row.

Row 13: K21, inc 1 st in next st, k4, inc 1 st in next st, k to end of row.

Row 15: K21, inc 1 st in next st, k6, inc 1 st in next st, k to end of row.

Row 17: K3, work row 1 of mitt graph, k3, inc 1 st in next st, k8, inc 1 st in next st, k to end of row.

Row 18: P32, work row 2 of mitt graph, p to end of row.

Row 19: K3, work row 3 of graph, k3, inc 1 st in next st, k10, inc 1 st in next st, k to end of row.

Row 20: P34, work row 4 of graph, p to end of row, 52 sts now on needle.

To make thumb:

K3, work row 5 of graph, k17, turn.

Next row: Cast on 1 st, p cast-on st and next 13 sts, turn.

Next row: Cast on 1 st, k cast-on st and next 14 sts. Continue even in St st on these 15 sts for 2 1/4 ins (6.0 cm), ending with right side facing for next row.

Next row: K1, (k2tog) to end of row. Break yarn. Thread end through rem sts. Draw up and fasten securely. Sew thumb seam.

To make remainder of mitt:

With right side of work facing, join yarn to last st on right-hand needle. Pick up and k 2 sts at base of thumb.

K across sts on left-hand needle.

Next row: P22, working 2 sts picked up at base of thumb together (counts as 1 st), work row 6 of graph, p to end of row. Keeping continuity of graphed motif as established, work even in St st until work from ribbing measures 6 ins (15.0 cm), ending with right side facing for next row.

To shape top:

Continue work to end of graph at same time work as follows:

Row 1: K1, sl 1, k1, psso, k14, k2tog, k2, sl 1, k1, psso, k to last 3 sts, k2tog, k1.

Row 2: Purl.

Row 3: K1, sl 1, k1, psso, k12, k2tog, k2, sl 1, k1, psso, k to last 3 sts, k2tog, k1.

Row 4: Purl.

Row 5: K1, sl 1, k1, psso, k10, k2tog, k2,sl 1, k1, psso, k to last 3 sts, k2tog, k1.

Row 6: Purl.

Continue dec in this manner, having 2 sts less between dec on every alternate row to 16 sts on needle. Cast off purlways. Sew top and side seams.

Left mitt:

Work as for right mitt from **to**

Row 9: K16, inc 1 st in each of next 2 sts, k to end of row.

Rows 10, 12, 14 and 16: Purl.

Row 11: K16, inc 1 st in next st, k2, inc 1 st in next st, k to end of row.

Row 13: K16, inc 1 st in next st, k4, inc 1 st in next st, k to end of row.

Row 15: K16, inc 1 st in next st, k6, inc 1 st in next st, k to end of row.

Row 17: K16, inc 1 st in next st, k8, inc 1 st in next st, k5, work row 1 of mitt graph, k to end of row.

Row 18: P3, work row 2 of mitt graph, p to end of row.

Row 19: K16, inc 1 st in next st, k10, inc 1 st in next st, k5, work row 3 of mitt graph, k to end of row.

Row 20: P3, work row 4 of mitt graph, p to end of row. 52 sts now on needle.

To make thumb:

K30, turn.

Next row: Cast on 1 st, p cast-on st and next 13 sts, turn.

Next row: Cast on 1 st, k cast-on st and next 14 sts, turn.

Complete thumb as for right mitt.

To make remainder of mitt:

With right side of work facing join, yarn to last st on right-hand needle.

Next row: Pick up and k 2 sts at base of thumb, k4, work row 6 of mitt graph, k to end of row.

Next row: P3, work row 7 of graph, p to end of row, working 2 sts picked up at base of thumb together.

Complete remainder of mitt as for right mitt.

TO FINISH:

With crochet hook, make a chain 72 ins (183.0 cm) long. Sew ends of chain to mitts.

HEADBAND GRAPH

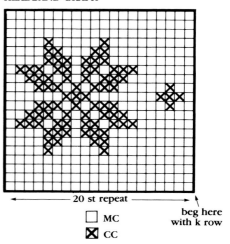

← 20 st repeat →

☐ MC
☒ CC

beg here
with k row

MITT GRAPH

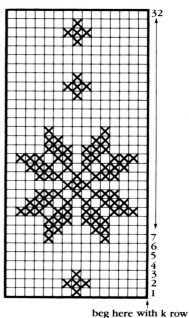

beg here with k row

Knitted Pocket People

The basic method for knitting these dolls is simple. Beginning at feet, knit a rectangle, shaping at top for the head. When body is sewn together and stuffed, arms and legs are defined by stitching through all layers.

YOU NEED

- **Small quantities of Sayelle or similar weight yarn in a variety of colors, including flesh tone**
- **One pair U.S. size 3 (3.00 mm) needles**
- **U.S. size D (3.00 mm) crochet hook**
- **Tapestry needle**
- **Embroidery floss**
- **Polyester fiberfill**

Note: Work pants in stripes, changing color every second row, and work pullover in solid color St st, or vice versa.

See General Directions (page 130) for knitting abbreviations.

Cast on 32 sts.

Knit one row, purl one row in same color for feet.

K 24 rows for pants.

Next row (beg hands row): K9 for pants, k3 in flesh tone, k8 for pants, k3 in flesh tone, k9 for pants.

Next row: K8 for pants, p4 in flesh tone, k8 for pants, p4 in flesh tone, k8 for pants.

Next row: K8 for pullover, k4 in flesh tone, k8 for pullover, k4 in flesh tone, k8 for pullover.

Next row: P8 for pullover, p4 in flesh tone, p8 for pullover, p4 in flesh tone, p8 for pullover.

Continue working 14 rows in St st for pullover.

Change to flesh tone and work 15 rows in St st for head as follows:

Rows 1 to 8: Work even in St st.

Row 9: Dec 5 sts evenly across row. 27 sts now on needle.
Row 10: Purl.
Row 11: Dec 5 sts evenly across row. 22 sts now on needle.
Row 12: Purl.
Row 13: Dec 5 sts evenly across row. 17 sts now on needle.
Row 14: Purl.
Row 15: K1, (K2tog) 8 times. Draw yarn through rem sts and pull up.

TO FINISH:

1. Sew sides together to form center back seam.

2. Stuff head. Weave a single strand of matching yarn through first head row. Draw up to form neck and tie tightly.

3. Stuff body and sew bottom opening closed.

4. With matching yarn, define arms by sewing small backstitches through all layers from waist to 3 rows below neckline. Define legs in the same manner from bottom edge to just below waistline.

5. For hair, cut 4 in. (10.0 cm) lengths of yarn. Attach hair to head as follows: With two strands together, fold in half to form a loop. Insert crochet hook into stitch on head, pull hair loop through stitch, and then pull yarn ends through loop. Fluff out hair and trim as desired.

6. Using three strands of floss, embroider eyes and mouth on face.

Pinecone Teddies

Design by Mary Corcoran

YOU NEED

For small bear:
- Four spruce or balsam cones
- Two mugho or red pinecones
- Two leaves cut from white pinecone
- 8 in. (approx. 20.5 cm) red ribbon, 1/4 in. (0.6 cm) wide
- 12 in. (30.5 cm) red thread
- Glue gun and glue
- Pruning shears

For tiny bear:
- Four tamarack or balsam cones
- Two spruce cones
- Two leaves cut from white pinecone
- 6 in. (approx. 15.0 cm) red ribbon, 1/8 in. (0.3 cm) wide
- 9 in. (approx. 23.0 cm) red thread

1. Select largest cone for body, medium cone for head and small cones for arms and legs. Lay on table. With base of cones at back, fit leaves of head cone into body cone. Glue together, holding in place until set.

2. Cones for arms and legs can be cut smaller, if desired. Glue in place.

3. Fit two white pinecone leaves in between leaves of head for ears. Glue in place.

4. To hang, fold thread in half. Knot ends. Loop around bear's neck.

5. Tie a ribbon bow. Glue at front neck. Trim ends.

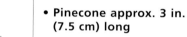

Pinecone Ornament

Design by Mary Corcoran

YOU NEED

- Pinecone approx. 3 in. (7.5 cm) long
- 7 in. (approx. 18.0 cm) florist ribbon, 1/2 in. (1.3 cm) wide
- Small decorations such as artificial greenery and fruit
- Glue gun or white craft glue
- Spray varnish

Varnish pinecone. Allow to dry thoroughly. Overlap and glue ends of ribbon together to form a loop. Glue loop to top of pinecone. Glue greenery and decorations in place inside ribbon loop at top of pinecone.

Pipe-Cleaner Clown

YOU NEED

- Bright colored calico, one piece 12 x 8 in. (30.0 x 20.0 cm) and a strip 7 x 1 1/4 in. (18.0 x 3.0 cm)
- Circle of white fine-knit fabric, 2 3/8 in. (6.0 cm) in diameter
- 1/4 yd. (0.25 m) white lace, approx. 3/4 in. (2.0 cm) wide
- 1/8 yd. (0.10 m) satin ribbon, 1/4 in. (0.6 cm) wide
- Three pipe cleaners, each 6 in. (15.0 cm) long
- Cotton ball
- Small scraps of red and black felt
- Small amount of Sayelle yarn for hair
- Matching thread
- Black thread
- White craft glue
- Brown paper

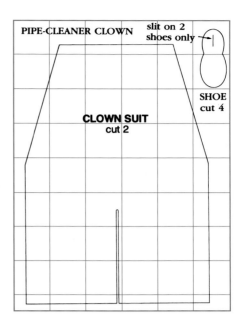

PIPE-CLEANER CLOWN

slit on 2 shoes only

CLOWN SUIT cut 2

SHOE cut 4

To enlarge pattern, see General Directions (page 130).

1. **Body:** Twist two pipe cleaners together at one end for 1/2 in. (1.3 cm), then make one twist at center point. Spread untwisted ends apart for legs and bend top section out in shape of a circle for body.

2. **Head:** Run a gathering thread around outer edge of knit fabric circle. Place cotton ball and top of pipe-cleaner body in center of fabric and pull up thread so cotton ball and end of pipe cleaners are completely enclosed. Secure thread ends. Using black thread, stitch a cross for each eye. Cut out and glue on a 1/4 in. (0.6 cm) circle of red felt for nose. Using yarn, stitch hair by taking small loops over top and back of head.

3. **Suit:** Cut two clown suit pieces from large piece of calico. With right sides together and using a 1/4 in. (0.6 cm) seam allowance, stitch up sides and around crotch. Press. Turn right-side out. Press under 1/2 in. (1.3 cm) at neck and ankle edges. Slip onto pipe-cleaner body. Run a gathering thread around neck edge of suit and draw up tightly. Secure thread ends. Gather ankle edges around legs in same manner, allowing legs to extend 1/2 in. beyond fabric for feet. Run a gathering thread around one edge of lace to form neck ruffle. Stitch securely in place around neck.

4. **Shoes:** Cut four shoes from black felt. Cut a small slit in two shoes as indicated on pattern. Glue one shoe with slit to one shoe without slit, inserting pipe-cleaner foot in slit so it is sandwiched between two layers. Repeat for other shoe and foot.

5. **Arms:** Press under 1/2 in. (1.3 cm) at short ends of calico strip. Fold strip in half so right sides are together and long edges meet. Stitch long edges together using a 1/4 in. (0.6 cm) seam allowance. Turn right-side out. Insert remaining pipe cleaner through this tube, gathering up fabric so pipe cleaner arm extends 1/2 in. beyond fabric at each end for hands. Slipstitch in place across back of clown just below neck ruffle.

6. Attach ribbon bow and hanging thread to top of head. Bend body in desired pose.

Cuddly Teddy

Design by Mary Corcoran

YOU NEED

- **Pieces of fake fur, 8 x 7 in. (20.5 x 18.0 cm) for body and 14 x 4 in. (35.5 x 10.0 cm) for arms, legs and ears**
- **Red felt, 14 x 3/4 in. (35.5 x 2.0 cm)**
- **Two snap-on glass eyes, approx. 3/8 in. (1.1 cm) in diameter**
- **Two red pom-poms, 5/8 in. (1.6 cm) in diameter**
- **One red pipe cleaner**
- **Matching thread**

- **Red and dark brown embroidery floss or pearl cotton**
- **Embroidery needle**
- **Polyester fiberfill**
- **Sharp scissors**
- **Dressmaker's chalk**
- **Knitting needle**
- **Glue gun and glue**
- **Brown paper**

Note: Stitch seams first, then cut, leaving a 1/4 in. (0.6 cm) seam allowance. Backstitch at beginning and end of seams.

To enlarge pattern, see General Directions (page 130).

1. Fold body fabric in half so right sides are together and short edges meet. Pin at corners. Lay pattern on fold (see Diagram 1). Using dressmaker's chalk, trace outline and placement markings. Do not cut out.

2. With point of scissors, make two small eyeholes in face. Insert eye shanks. Push on metal backings on wrong side.

3. With right sides together, fold fabric for arms, legs and ears in half so long edges meet. Pin at corners. Lay pattern pieces along fold (see Diagram 2), leaving a 1/4 in. (0.6 cm) seam allowance around each piece. Trace outline and markings. Do not cut out.

4. Stitch along all drawn outlines, being sure to leave base of body open. Cut out each piece leaving 1/4 in. (0.6 cm) allowance outside stitching lines.

Cut ears, arm and leg pieces in half along lines indicated. Clip corners. Turn all pieces right-side out.

5. Stuff body firmly using knitting needle to push in small bits of fiberfill. Stuff legs and arms firmly at ends and less firmly toward opening.

6. Using doubled thread, slipstitch open end of ears in place at sides of head. Slipstitch arms and legs to body in the same manner. Slipstitch opening at base of bear closed.

7. Using embroidery floss and satin stitch, embroider brown nose and red mouth.

8. For earmuffs, cut a 3 1/4 in. (8.5 cm) length of pipe cleaner. Glue pom-poms to each end of pipe cleaner and then glue ends to either side of head in front of ears.

9. For scarf, cut a fringe at each end of felt strip. Tie around neck of bear.

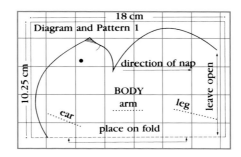

Diagram and Pattern 1

18 cm

10.25 cm

direction of nap

BODY

arm   leg   leave open

ear

place on fold

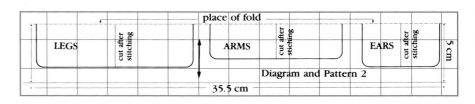

place of fold

LEGS   cut after stitching   ARMS   cut after stitching   EARS   cut after stitching   5 cm

Diagram and Pattern 2

35.5 cm

Snowman, Duck, Angel and Santa

Designs by Renée Schwarz

Finished ornaments are approx. 3 1/4 to 3 1/2 in. (8.0 to 9.0 cm) high.

YOU NEED

- **Piece of white sweat-suit fleece, 11 x 5 1/2 in. (28.0 x 14.0 cm), for body, head and arms**
- **Piece of blue sweat-suit fleece, 6 x 3 1/2 in. (15.0 x 9.0 cm), for hat**
- **Scrap of orange cotton fabric, for nose**
- **Black embroidery floss**
- **Matching thread**
- **Invisible nylon thread**
- **Polyester fiberfill**
- **Small twig**
- **Brown paper**

Note: Use a 1/4 in. (0.6 cm) seam allowance throughout, unless otherwise indicated. Backstitch at beginning and end of all seams. Sew fabric with right sides together, unless otherwise indicated.

For full-size pattern pieces, see pages 136 and 137.

SNOWMAN

1. **Head:** From white fleece, cut two head sides and one head back. Sew two side pieces together, leaving open at bottom as indicated. Open up and pin to head back, matching points A. Stitch, leaving a 1 in. (2.5 cm) opening at bottom as indicated. Turn right-side out. Stuff firmly. Slipstitch opening closed.

2. **Body:** From white fleece, cut two body sides and one body bottom. Stitch and stuff as for head. With floss, embroider three buttons down center front seam, 1/4 in. (0.6 cm) apart.

3. **Nose:** Cut nose from orange fabric. Fold in half lengthwise so right sides are together. Stitch from A to B. Turn right-side out. Stuff.

4. **Face:** Using two strands of floss, embroider eyes (satin stitch) on either side of center front head seam, outlining each with backstitch. Turn under 1/8 in. (0.3 cm) at open end of nose and slipstitch in place on face. With single strand of floss, embroider small Xs for mouth. Hand-stitch head securely to top of body.

5. **Arms:** From white fleece, cut four arms. Stitch two arms together, leaving open at straight end. Turn right-side out. Stuff. Make second arm in same manner. Turn under 1/4 in. (0.6 cm) at open end of each arm and slipstitch securely to sides of body, approx. 3/4 in. (2.0 cm) from buttons.

6. **Hat:** Cut hat from blue fleece. Fold in half as indicated and stitch, leaving open at bottom. Turn right-side out. Turn under 1/4 in. (0.6 cm) around open edge and slipstitch in place on head. Fold tip of hat down and tack.

7. Sew twig to one arm with invisible thread. Thread hanging loop of invisible thread through top of hat.

DUCK

1. **Head:** Cut pieces from yellow fleece and assemble as for Snowman, Step 1.

2. **Body:** Cut pieces from yellow fleece and assemble as for Snowman, Step 2.

3. **Beak:** Cut two beaks from red fleece. Stitch together using a 1/8 in. (0.3 cm) seam allowance and leaving open at straight end. Turn right-side out. Turn under 1/8 in. at open end.

4. **Face:** Using two strands of floss, embroider eyes (satin stitch) 1 1/4 in. (3.0 cm) down from top of head on either side of center front seam, outlining each with backstitch. Slipstitch beak in place just below eyes. Hand-stitch head securely to top of body.

5. **Wings:** From yellow fleece, cut four wings. Stitch two wings together, leaving open at straight end. Turn right-side out. Stuff. Make second wing in same manner. Turn under 1/4 in. (0.6 cm) at open end of each wing and slipstitch securely to sides of body.

6. **Tall:** Cut two tails from yellow fleece. Assemble as for wing and slipstitch to back of body approx. 3/4 in. (2.0 cm) from bottom.

7. **Hat:** Cut piece from red fleece and assemble as for Snowman, Step 6.

8. Crochet a scarf approx 3/8 in. (1.0 cm) wide and 6 in. (15.0 cm) long. Attach a fringe to both ends of scarf. Tie around bird's neck. Thread hanging loop of invisible thread through top of hat.

Cute little ducks bundled up in colorful scarves and tuques.

ANGEL

1. **Head:** Cut pieces from beige fleece and assemble as for Snowman, Step 1.

2. **Body:** Cut angel body and body bottom from white fleece. Fold body in half and stitch straight edges together from A to B. Open up at wide end and stitch to body bottom. Turn right-side out. Stuff firmly.

3. **Face and trim:** Using two strands of navy floss, embroider eyes (satin stitch) 1 1/4 in. (3.0 cm) down from top of head on either side of center front seam, outlining each with backstitch. With single strand of brown floss, embroider a small circle for nose just below eyes. With a single strand of red floss, embroider mouth using backstitch. Turn under 1/4 in. (0.6 cm) at open end of body and hand-stitch head securely to top of body. Hand-stitch lace around neck and bottom of body. Wind bouclé yarn around head for hair and tack in place with matching thread. Bend silver cord into a circle and stitch to back of head to form halo.

4. **Wings:** Cut four wings from eyelet and two from fabric stiffener. Place stiffener between two eyelet pieces and satin-stitch around outer edge. Repeat for second wing. Slipstitch wings to back of body, 1/4 in. (0.6 cm) from center back seam.

5. Thread hanging loop of invisible thread through top of head.

SANTA

1. **Head:** Cut pieces from beige fleece and assemble as for Snowman, Step 1.

2. **Body:** Cut pieces from red fleece and assemble as for Snowman, Step 2. With black floss, embroider two buttons down center front seam. Hand-stitch bias tape around body for belt, just below buttons. Cut belt buckle from yellow fabric. Turn under 1/4 in. (0.6 cm) on all edges and hand-stitch in place on belt, just under buttons.

3. **Face:** Using two strands of floss, embroider eyes (satin stitch) 1 1/4 in. (3.0 cm) down from top of head on either side of center front seam, outlining each with backstitch. Embroider red nose just below eyes in same manner. With a single strand of red floss, embroider mouth using backstitch. Hand-stitch head securely to top of body. Wrap bouclé yarn around face for hair and beard and tack in place with matching thread.

4. **Arms:** From red fleece, cut two arms, and from blue fleece, cut two hands. Stitch hand to arm. Fold in half so long edges meet and right sides are together. Stitch, leaving open at straight end. Turn right-side out. Stuff. Make second arm in same manner. Turn under 1/4 in. (0.6 cm) at open end of each arm and slipstitch securely to sides of body.

5. **Hat:** Cut piece from red fleece and assemble as for Snowman, Step 6.

6. Thread hanging loop of invisible thread through top of hat.

Glitzen the Sock Reindeer

YOU NEED

- **Man's work sock, with contrasting-color heel and toe**
- **1/2 yd. (0.40 m) red calico, 45 in. (approx. 115.0 cm) wide**
- **1/4 yd. (0.25 m) each of five different printed and plain green cotton fabrics, 45 in. (115.0 cm) wide, for holly leaves**
- **Piece of green cotton or broadcloth, approx. 17 3/4 x 13 3/4 in. (45.0 x 35.0 cm), for back piece**
- **2 1/4 yd. (2.00 m) gold braid, edged with red, 5/8 in. (1.6 cm) wide**
- **1 1/8 yd. (1.00 m) green satin ribbon, 7/8 in. (2.2 cm) wide**
- **1 1/8 yd. (1.00 m) green satin ribbon, 1/2 in. (1.2 cm) wide**
- **Small scraps of red and black felt**
- **Two gold buttons, 1/2 in. (1.3 cm) in diameter**
- **Pair of plastic eyelashes (available at craft supply stores)**
- **Red pom-pom, 5/8 in. (1.6 cm) in diameter**
- **Polyester fiberfill**
- **Fabric glue (optional)**
- **Matching thread**
- **Heavy thread**
- **Brown paper**

Note: Use a 1/4 in. (0.6 cm) seam allowance throughout, unless otherwise indicated. When sewing antler, leaf and back pieces together, use a closely spaced machine stitch.

To enlarge pattern, see General Directions (page 130).

1. Turn sock inside out. Measure sock length from heel to toe. If longer than 9 in. (23.0 cm), machine-stitch a tuck around sock, approx 7 in. (18.0 cm) from toe, to make correct length. Turn sock right-side out. Stuff firmly with fiberfill to within 3 1/8 in. (8.0 cm) of opening. With heavy thread, tie opening tightly closed. Wrap wide green ribbon around closing and tie in a large bow at front.

2. **Harness:** Pin a length of gold braid around nose, covering tuck seam, so that ends overlap 5/8 in. (1.5 cm). Turn under 1/4 in. (0.6 cm) along top overlap. Slipstitch braid in place.

Reins: Cut remaining gold braid in half. Turn under 1/4 in. (0.6 cm) along one end of each piece. Pin each folded end to harness at each side of head. Pin each rein straight back along side of head and around to center back, aligning top edge of braid with edge of contrasting-color heel. Slipstitch in place. Reinforce stitching at center back where two reins meet. To make hanging loop, tie loose ends of reins in a bow approx. 13 7/8 in. (35.0 cm) from join at center back.

3. **Face:** From red felt, cut heart for mouth. Stitch or glue in place on end of nose. Center pom-pom above mouth. Stitch or glue in place. With heavy thread, stitch button eyes and lashes in place. From black felt, cut two eyelids. Fit eyelids over lashes, cupping slightly. Stitch or glue in place.

4. **Antlers:** From red calico, cut four antlers. With right sides of two pieces together, stitch, leaving bottom edges open. Carefully trim seam allowances to 1/8 in. (0.3 cm). Turn right-side out. Stuff firmly. Turn under 1/4 in. (0.6 cm) around openings. Using heavy thread, stitch antlers to top of head. Tack antlers together at X. Cut narrow green ribbon in half. Wrap one length of ribbon around base of each antler. Tie in a bow.

5. **Leaves:** From green cotton, cut thirty holly leaves (six from each 1/4 yd. (0.25 m) length of fabric). With right sides of two pieces together, stitch, leaving bottom edge open. Carefully trim seam allowance to 1/8 in. (0.3 cm). Turn right-side out. Stuff lightly. Turn under 1/4 in. (0.6 cm) around opening. Edgestitch opening closed. Machine-quilt center line of leaf indicated by dotted line. Make fourteen more leaves in same manner.

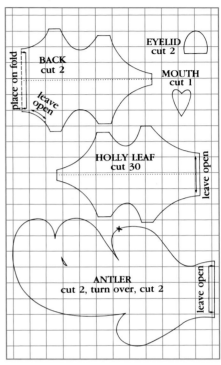

GLITZEN, THE SOCK REINDEER

EYELID
cut 2

BACK
cut 2

MOUTH
cut 1

place on fold

leave open

HOLLY LEAF
cut 30

leave open

ANTLER
cut 2, turn over, cut 2

leave open

6. **Back:** From green cotton, cut two back pieces. With right sides together, stitch, leaving open between notches on one half. Carefully trim seam allowance to 1/8 in. (0.3 cm). Turn right-side out. Stuff lightly. Turn under 1/8 in. around opening. Slipstitch opening closed. Machine-quilt center line indicated by dotted line.

7. Arrange holly leaves on back, having bottom straight edges toward center. Hand-stitch in place. Center reindeer head on top of leaves. Using heavy thread, hand-stitch in place. Tack antlers to leaves, if necessary.

Candy-Cane Clown

Design by Renée Schwarz

The finished clown is approx. 14 1/2 in. (37.0 cm) tall.

YOU NEED

- **1/4 (0.15 m) red-and-white-striped fabric, approx. 45 in. (115.0 cm) wide**
- **Piece of flesh-tone broadcloth, 11 x 7 1/2 in. (28.0 x 19.0 cm)**
- **Piece of red broad-cloth, 21 1/4 x 4 1/4 in. (54.0 x 11.0 cm)**
- **Small scrap of yellow fabric**

- **1/2 yd. (0.45 m) narrow red rickrack**
- **Navy, red and yellow embroidery floss**
- **1 1/8 in. (3.0 cm) white elastic, 1/4 in. (0.6 cm) wide**
- **Green crochet cotton yarn**
- **Matching thread**
- **Polyester fiberfill**
- **Brown paper**

Note: Use a 1/4 in. (0.6 cm) seam allowance unless otherwise indicated. Backstitch at beginning and end of all seams.

To enlarge pattern, see General Directions (page 130).

1. **Head:** Cut head gusset and two head pieces from flesh-tone broadcloth. Trace facial markings onto one head piece only. With right sides together, stitch one side of gusset to one head piece, then other side of gusset to second head piece. Turn right-side out. Stuff firmly. Using two strands of floss, embroider (satin stitch) navy eyes, red nose, yellow cheeks and red mouth, outlining each with backstitch.

2. From striped fabric, cut four legs, two arms, one front, two backs and two hats, being sure to flip pattern pieces where indicated. From red cotton, cut two hands and four feet. **Arms:** With right sides together, pin

hand to arm from A to B, taking two small tucks in arm about 5/8 in. (1.5 cm) from each edge to fit. Stitch. Fold arm/hand in half lengthwise so right sides are together. Stitch around hand with red thread and up arm with white thread, leaving top open. Clip curves. Turn right-side out. Stuff hand firmly and arm slightly less firmly. Make second arm/hand in same manner.

3. **Legs:** With right sides together, pin foot to leg from A to B, taking a small tuck at center of leg to fit. Stitch. Repeat with other three foot and leg pieces. With right sides of two foot/legs together, stitch around foot with red thread and up leg with white thread, leaving top

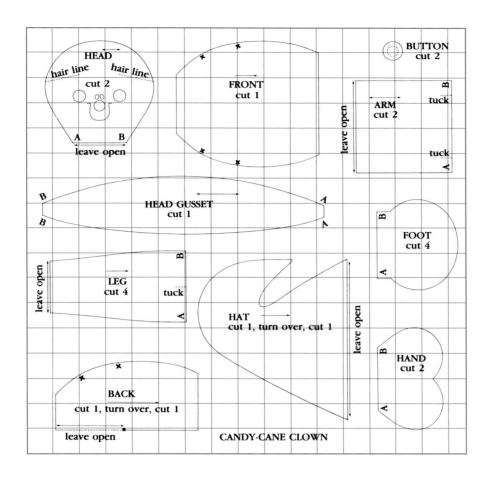

open. Clip curves. Turn right-side out. Stuff foot firmly and leg slightly less firmly. Make second foot/leg in same manner.

4. **Body:** With right sides of backs together, stitch from bottom edge to small dot. Pin front to back, placing top of arms between front and back between Xs so underarm seam faces down. Allow top of arm to project 3/8 in. (1.0 cm) past edge of body. Stitch side seams, reinforcing with a second row of stitching over arms. Turn body right-side out. Turn under 3/8 in. around opening at bottom of body. Insert top of legs. Topstitch in place twice. Turn under 1/4 in. (0.6 cm) around neck edge. Sew rickrack around neck edge. Pin neck to head and slipstitch securely in place. Stuff body. Turn under 1/4 in. on back opening edge. Fold elastic in half to form a loop and sew at top of back opening. Clown may be suspended from this hanging loop. Slipstitch back opening closed.

5. **Hair:** Wrap green yarn around a 6 x 1 in. (15.0 x 2.5 cm) strip of paper. Stitch 1/4 in. (0.6 cm) from one long edge. Cut loops along opposite long edge. Tear away paper, and cut fringe in half. Hand-stitch in place on either side of head along broken line indicated on pattern.

6. **Hat:** With right sides of hat together, stitch around curved edge, leaving open at bottom. Clip curves. Turn right-side out. Turn under 1/4 in. (0.6 cm) around bottom edge. Sew rickrack around bottom edge. Slipstitch securely to head.

7. Cut two small circles from yellow fabric for buttons. Turn under edge of each to form a 3/8 in. (1.0 cm) circle. Sew circles to front of clown using tiny hand stitches.

Spritely Elf

DESIGN BY CHRISTINE McCORMACK

A beaming little red, white and green elf will help make any bazaar a resounding success. Sew several of them, and see how their happy faces and jingle bells turn on the holiday smiles.

YOU NEED

- 1/4 yd. (0.20 m) green felt, 72 in. (180.0 cm) wide
- 1/2 yd. (0.40 m) red-and-white-striped fabric, approx. 45 in. (115.0 cm) wide
- Piece of white flannelette, 16 x 12 in. (40.0 x 30.0 cm)
- Scraps of white, red, green and black felt
- Matching threads
- Shank button, 3/8 in. (1.0 cm) in diameter
- Three jingle bells
- Polyester fiberfill
- Brown paper

Note: Use a 1/4 in. (0.6 cm) seam allowance throughout.

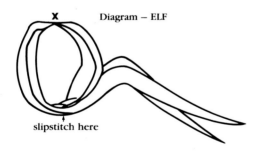

Diagram — ELF

x

slipstitch here

To enlarge pattern, see General Directions (page 130).

1. Cut body/legs from green felt, head from flannelette and arms and hat from striped fabric. Cut eyes, ears, cheeks, holly leaves and berries from color of felt indicated on pattern.

2. **Body/legs:** Stitch two body/leg pieces together from A, around one leg to B, then around other leg to C. Leave open at end. Trim seam allowance. Cut along slash line between legs. Turn right-side out. Stuff, using a chopstick to poke fiberfill into legs. Stuff slightly less around fold areas. Turn under 1/4 in. (0.6 cm) at open end. Slipstitch closed. Sew bell to tip of each foot.

3. **Arms:** With right sides folded together, stitch raw edge of arms together, leaving a 2 in. (5.0 cm) opening at center of long edge. Trim seam allowance. Turn right-side out. Stuff. Slipstitch opening closed.

4. **Hat:** With right sides together, stitch hat pieces together along long edges. Turn right-side out. Turn under 1/4 in. (0.6 cm) on bottom edge. Hem. Stitch bell to tip of hat.

5. **Head:** With right sides together, stitch two head pieces together on one edge. Open out. With right sides together, stitch third piece to the first two pieces, leaving a 2 in. (5.0 cm) opening in one seam. Trim seam allowances. Turn right-side out. Stuff firmly to form round head. Slipstitch opening closed.

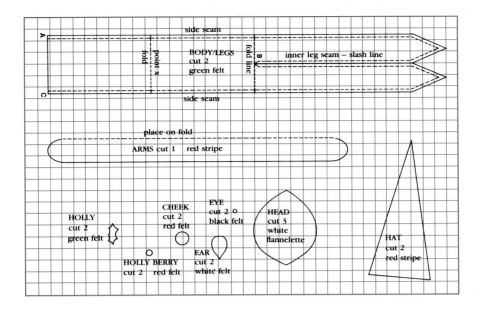

6. **Face:** From flannelette, cut a 7/8 in. (2.3 cm) diameter circle. Run a line of gathering stitches around edge. Place button in center. Pull up thread, enclosing button. Knot securely. Sew in place on face. Glue cheeks and eyes in place. Cut a smiling mouth from black felt and glue in place. Fit hat on head and tack to sides of head. Glue holly leaves and berries to hat. Stitch base of ears to sides of head, close to edge of hat.

7. Fold body along fold lines into shape shown in Diagram. Slipstitch end of body to top of legs. Slipstitch center of arms to inside of body loop at point X. Place head on top of X. Slipstitch in place. Bring arms around front of legs, just under knees. Overlap hands. Tack together. Tack hands to legs.

Finger Puppets

DESIGN BY NORENE SMILEY

This colorful cast of characters includes Santa, Mrs. Claus, Fairy Godmother, Princess, Clown, Wizard, Elf and Angel. Create a basketful of these easy-to-make puppets to sell at your bazaar, to give as gifts or to decorate your own tree.

YOU NEED

- Felt, approx. 8 in. (20.0 cm) square for each puppet body
- Scraps of felt in assorted colors
- Nylon stocking or pantyhose
- Matching threads
- Red embroidery floss
- Seed beads

- Assorted accessories and trims as follows: scraps of yarn for hair, Kurly Kate pot scrubber for fairy godmother's hair, chenille stem for fairy godmother's wand, feathers for angel's wings, jingle bell for Santa's hat
- Polyester fiberfill
- White craft glue
- Brown paper

To enlarge pattern pieces, see General Directions (page 130).

1. Cut body front and backs from felt. With wrong sides together, edgestitch one side of front to one back piece, then other side of front to other back piece between Xs. Edgestitch center back seam and down front peak, where appropriate.

MRS. CLAUS　　FAIRY GODMOTHER　　ELF　　CLOWN　　ANGEL　　SANTA　　PRINCESS　　WIZARD

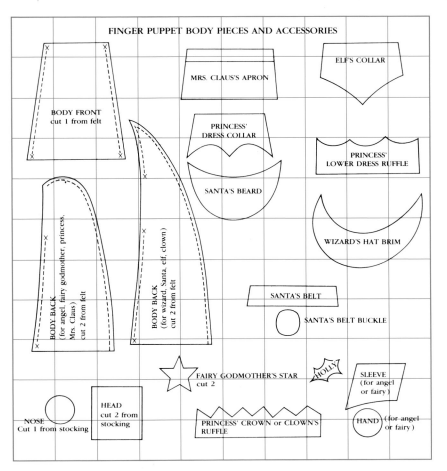

FINGER PUPPET BODY PIECES AND ACCESSORIES

BODY FRONT
cut 1 from felt

BODY BACK
(for angel, fairy godmother, princess, Mrs. Claus)
cut 2 from felt

BODY BACK
(for wizard, Santa, elf, clown)
cut 2 from felt

MRS. CLAUS'S APRON

PRINCESS' DRESS COLLAR

SANTA'S BEARD

ELF'S COLLAR

PRINCESS' LOWER DRESS RUFFLE

WIZARD'S HAT BRIM

SANTA'S BELT

SANTA'S BELT BUCKLE

FAIRY GODMOTHER'S STAR
cut 2

HOLLY

SLEEVE
(for angel or fairy)

NOSE
Cut 1 from stocking

HEAD
cut 2 from stocking

PRINCESS' CROWN or CLOWN'S RUFFLE

HAND (for angel or fairy)

2. From nylon stocking, cut two head pieces and one nose. Stitch head pieces together along three edges. Stuff with small pieces of fiberfill. Slipstitch opening closed. Run a line of gathering stitches around edge of nose. Place a tiny amount of fiberfill on wrong side. Pull up gathering thread to form a small ball. Knot thread. Slipstitch to middle of face. Sew on seed bead eyes, and embroider a red mouth. Pin head into body opening. Slipstitch in place.

3. Using Diagrams and photo as a guide, complete each puppet by sewing or gluing the appropriate felt accessories and hair in place. Decorate each with sequins, if desired.

Mr. and Mrs. Claus

DESIGN BY RENÉE SCHWARZ

Pleasantly plump Mr. and Mrs. Claus are so-o-o irresistible, they'll be sold out before you know it. Bespectacled Mrs. Claus wears a lacey white apron and Santa sports a jaunty red and white cap.

MR. CLAUS

Finished Santa is 5 1/2 in. (14.0 cm) high, and Mrs. Claus is 2 3/4 in. (7.0 cm) high. For full-size pattern pieces, see page 135.

Note: *Sew fabric with right sides together, using a 1/4 in. (0.6 cm) seam allowance throughout, unless otherwise indicated. Backstitch at beginning and end of all seams.*

For full-size pattern pieces, see page 135.

YOU NEED

- **Piece of red sweat-suit fleece, 11 x 8 in. (26.0 x 20.0 cm), for body front, back, bottom and hat**
- **Piece of white felt, 7 x 3 in. (18.0 x 7.0 cm), for beard and hat trim**
- **Piece of flesh-tone broadcloth, 2 3/4 x 2 in. (6.0 x 5.0 cm), for face**
- **White pom-pom, 5/8 in. (1.6 cm) in diameter**
- **Navy and red embroidery floss**
- **Matching threads**
- **Invisible nylon thread**
- **Polyester fiberfill**
- **Dressmaker's pencil**
- **Brown paper**

1. **Body:** From red fleece, cut two body backs, one body front and one bottom. Stitch two back pieces together along center back seam, leaving a 3/8 in. (1.0 cm) opening at top. Stitch body front to body back, leaving open at bottom and a 3/8 in. opening at top. Open up and pin to body bottom, matching Xs. Stitch. Turn right-side out. Stuff firmly. Turn under 1/4 in. (0.6 cm) at top. Slipstitch opening closed.

2. **Face:** Draw eyes and nose lightly on face fabric. Using a single strand of floss, embroider (satin stitch) eyes in navy and nose in red, outlining each with backstitch. Cut out face. Baste edge under 1/4 in. (0.6 cm).
Pin face to body front, so bottom edge of face is approx. 1 1/8 in. (3.0 cm) up from bottom seam. Slipstitch in place, inserting a bit of stuffing behind face before closing completely.

3. **Beard:** From white felt, cut two beards. Stitch beard pieces together, 1/8 in. (0.3 cm) from edge. Slipstitch beard around face and to body.

4. **Hat:** Cut hat from fleece. From felt, cut a 6 3/4 x 3/8 in. (17.0 x 1.0 cm) strip. Fold hat and stitch center back seam, leaving open at bottom. Turn right-side out. Turn under 1/4 in. (0.6 cm) around bottom edge and hem. Stitch felt strip around bottom of hat. Sew on pom-pom. Place hat on head, matching center back seams. Slipstitch in place.

5. Thread hanging loop of invisible thread through hat.

MRS. CLAUS

YOU NEED

- Piece of red fleece, 11 x 8 in. (26.0 x 20.0 cm) for body front, back, bottom and bonnet
- Piece of white broadcloth, 2 1/2 x 2 in. (6.5 x 5.0 cm), for apron
- Piece of flesh-tone broadcloth, 2 3/4 x 2 in. (6.0 x 5.0 cm), for face
- 1/4 yd. (0.20 m) white bias tape, 1/4 in. (0.6 cm) wide
- 1/2 yd. (0.45 m) white lace with scalloped edge, 3/8 in. (1.0 cm) wide
- One eye (i.e., hook and "eye"), 3/8 in. (1.0 cm) long, for glasses
- Navy, red and brown embroidery floss
- Matching threads
- Invisible nylon thread
- Polyester fiberfill
- Brown paper

1. **Body:** Cut pieces from red fleece and assemble as for Mr. Claus, Step 1.

2. **Face:** Embroider features (including brown nose and red mouth); cut face from broadcloth and assemble as for Mr. Claus, Step 2. Stitch glasses in place.

3. **Bonnet:** Cut bonnet from red fleece. Turn under 1/4 in. (0.6 cm) around edge. Run gathering thread around edge. Stitch lace in place, so scalloped edge extends 1/4 in. past edge. Pull up gathering thread, so hat fits head. Knot securely. Slipstitch hat to body.

4. **Apron:** Fold apron in half, so right sides are together and short edges meet. Stitch long edge and one short edge. Turn right-side out. Turn under 1/4 in. (0.6 cm) on open edge. Edgestitch around entire apron. Stitch lace to back and front of one long edge (bottom), so scalloped edge extends 1/8 in. (0.3 cm) past apron and ends overlap at back. Fold bias tape in half, so long edges meet. Stitch edges together. Slipstitch bias tape around body 5/8 in. (1.5 cm) above bottom seam so ends meet at center front. Slipstitch top of apron over bias tape, just under face.

5. Thread hanging loop of invisible thread through bonnet.

Santa with Attitude

DESIGN BY CAROL MOORE

Depending on your choice of fabric and what you opt to put in his arms, this chubby little Santa will take on any persona. Ready to party? Give him a mini martini glass. Sweet as could be? Tuck some bonbons into a sack. Au natural? Add a tiny wreath of berries.

YOU NEED

- **1/4 yd. 0.20 m) light-weight fabric (such as broadcloth, taffeta or vel-veteen), 45 in. (115 cm) wide**
- **Matching thread**
- **Small scrap of white muslin**
- **Small amount of white-washed sheep's fleece (available at weaving supply stores)**
- **Polyester fiberfill**
- **1 small jingle bell**
- **Pink lipstick**
- **Black permanent fine-tip felt marker**
- **Miniature ornament (such as a gift, teddy bear, wreath, wrapped candy or martini glass)**
- **Glue gun**

Note: Use a 1/4 in (0.6 cm) seam allowance throughout.

For pattern pieces, see page 138.

1. From lightweight fabric cut two bodies, one hat and one 6 x 1 3/4 in. (15.0 x 4.5 cm) rectangle for arms. From white muslin cut an oval measuring approx. 1 1/2 x 1 1/8 in. (4.0 x 3.0 cm) for face.

2. **Body:** With right sides together, stitch body front to body back, leaving open along bottom edge. Turn right side out. Stuff firmly. Turn under 1/4 in. (0.6 cm) around bottom edge and slipstitch closed. Glue white muslin oval to center front of head.

3. **Arms:** Fold long edges of arm piece under to form a strip approx 5/8 in. (1.5 cm) wide. Glue exposed raw edge in place. Position bottom edge of arm strip 4 in. (10.0 cm) up from bottom of body and pin each end of strip to body, just behind the side seam. Glue ends in place. Make an angled tuck in the arms at center front and secure with a dab of glue.

4. **Hat:** Lap one long edge of hat triangle over other long edge to form a cone. Glue seam. Sew or glue bell to point of hat. Glue bottom edge of hat to head, over-lapping upper part of face. Fluff out a piece of fleece and roll into a narrow band approx 5 1/8 in. (13.0 cm) long. Glue band around bottom edge of hat. Fold hat to one side and secure with a dab of glue.

5. **Beard and face:** Fluff out another piece of fleece to look like a beard. Glue in place around chin/neck area extending up to the hat trim on each side of face. With marker, make two small dots for eyes. Dab a little lip-stick on fingertip and dot lightly on face for rosy cheeks.

6. Tuck miniature ornament between arms and body or on top of arms. Glue in place.

Folk Art Angel

DESIGN BY JANE BUCKLES

Wooden Folk Art Angels can be mounted on sticks as mantel or tabletop decorations, or threaded with festive ribbons and hung as tree ornaments. Make several of each for folksy, handcrafted treasures to sell at a bazaar or save as stocking stuffers.

YOU NEED

- Scrap of pine, 6 3/4 x 2 1/2 x 1 in. (17.0 x 6.0 x 2.5 cm), for body and feet, and an additional piece, 5 x 2 1/2 x 1 in. (12.5 x 6.0 x 2.5 cm), for base of angel mounted on stand
- 3/8 in (1.0 cm) dowelling, 3 in. (7.5 cm) long, for legs, and an additional 6 1/4 in. (16.0 cm), for angel mounted on stand

- Round wooden hole plug, 1 in. (2.5 cm) diameter (available at most lumber and hardware stores)
- Tongue depressor
- 3/4 yd. (0.70 m) yarn, for hair
- 3 1/2 in. (9.0 cm) coat hanger wire, for halo
- Screw eye, for hanging angel only
- 1/2 yd. (0.45 m) ribbon

- Heavy white construction paper, watercolor paper or Bristol board
- Flesh-tone, red and blue colored pencils
- Black permanent fine-tip felt marker
- White and gold paint
- Small artist's paintbrush
- Iron-on metal stars and dots (available at craft and sewing supply stores)

- White craft glue
- Saw
- Electric drill with 1 in. (25.4 mm), 3/8 in. (9.525 mm) and 1/8 in. (3.175 mm) bits
- Pliers
- X-ACTO knife
- Sandpaper
- Brown paper

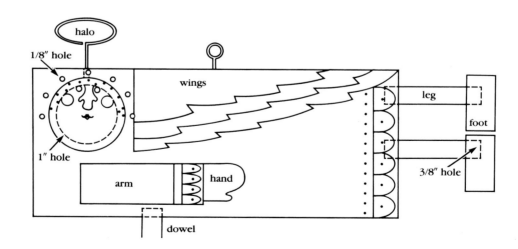

1. Cut larger piece of pine into one piece 6 x 2 1/2 in. (15.0 x 6.0 cm) for body and two pieces 1 x 3/4 in. (2.5 x 2.0 cm) for feet. Cut dowelling in half for legs. From tongue depressor, cut a 2 in. (5.0 cm) length for arm. Sand all pieces lightly.

2. Bend one end of wire into a 1 in. (2.5 cm) diameter circle and other end straight down to form stem of halo. Paint halo gold.

3. Referring to Diagram opposite, drill a 1 in. (25.4 mm) hole in front of body for face, two 3/8 in. (9.525 mm) holes in opposite end of body for legs, one 3/8 in. hole in each foot to fit legs, seven 1/8 in. (3.175 mm) holes around face for hair and one 1/8 in. hole in top of block above face for halo.

4. From paper, cut out two of each wing layer and one hand (shown actual size on page 137). Referring to Diagram, glue one set of wings one layer on top of the other to front of body, and the other set to back. Glue arm and hand in place.

5. Glue plug in face hole and legs into body and feet.

6. Color face with flesh-tone pencil. Draw features with marker and other pencils. Rub with finger to soften look, if necessary. Paint all other parts white. Paint decorative dots, stars and wavy lines on body with gold paint, or decorate with iron-on shapes following manufacturer's directions for ironing onto fabric.

7. Cut yarn into seven 4 in. (10.0 cm) lengths. Fold each in half. Dab glue on fold and poke into each hole around face with nail or darning needle. When glue is dry, trim hair. Glue halo in hole in top of head.

8. To hang angel, insert screw eye into center top of body, thread loop of ribbon through it and tie in a bow. To mount angel on base, omit screw eye. Drill one 3/8 in. (9.575 mm) hole in bottom of block under arm and another in base. Glue and insert extra dowel in holes. Tie ribbon bow around base of dowel.

CHAPTER 6

Dolls and
Toys to Make

Paws

DESIGN BY ANNA HOBBS

Paws is a cuddly armful of adorable bear to create for that special child who'll give him lots of love. He's fake fur on the outside, and inside he's all heart and polyester fiberfill. A minimum number of pattern pieces make Paws an easy-to-sew project.

YOU NEED

- 7/8 yd. (0.80 m) beige fake fur, 56 in. (140.0 cm) wide
- Piece of dark brown felt, 10 in. (25.0 cm) square
- Scrap of black felt
- Matching thread
- 1 1/8 yd. (1.00 m) dark brown yarn
- 1 1/8 yd. (1.00 m) ribbon, 1 in. (2.5 cm) wide
- Polyester fiberfill
- Water-soluble fabric marker
- White craft glue
- Brown paper

Note: Use a 1/2 in. (1.3 cm) seam allowance throughout.

For pattern pieces, see page 138. To enlarge pattern pieces, see General Directions (page 130).

1. From brown felt, cut two paws, two soles and two large eye circles. From black felt, cut two small eye circles.

2. Place remaining pattern pieces on wrong side of single thickness of fake fur, positioning each piece so arrow runs in direction of nap. To determine direction of nap, stroke fur in whichever direction will make it lie flat and feel smoothest. Trace around pattern pieces with marker, being careful to reverse pattern pieces for arms and legs. Cut out pieces. Use tip of scissors only to snip through fabric backing, being careful not to cut fur on right side.

3. Topstitch felt paw pads in place on fur side of one right and one left arm. With right sides together, stitch arm pieces together in pairs, leaving open at top. Trim seam allowances. Clip curves. Turn right-side out. Stuff arms firmly to within 1 in. (2.5 cm) of top. Machine-stitch closed.

4. With right sides together, stitch leg pieces together in pairs down center front and center back seams. With right sides together and notches matching leg seams, stitch felt sole to bottom of each foot. Trim seam allowances. Clip corners and curves. Turn right-side out. Stuff legs firmly to within 1 in. (2.5 cm) of top. Fold top of leg so that front and back seams align. Machine-stitch closed.

5. With right sides together, stitch ear pieces together in pairs, leaving open where indicated. Trim seam allowances. Clip curves. Turn right-side out. Do not stuff. Baste raw edges together, pulling thread up slightly to gather edge.

6. With raw edges even, baste ears to right side of body front where indicated. With right sides together, stitch body front to body back from one shoulder, around head to opposite shoulder, catching ears in stitching. Insert arms between front and back body so raw end of each arm is even with raw edge of side seam and so paws point upward. Stitch side seams, catching arms in stitching.

7. With right sides together and toes pointing away from body, stitch raw end of legs to bottom edge of body back. Turn body right-side out. Stuff head and body firmly, filling out cheeks and shoulders as much as possible. Slipstitch bottom opening closed.

8. **Snout:** Run a line of gathering stitches around edge of snout circle. Place a handful of fiberfill on wrong side. Pull up gathering thread, adjusting stuffing to form a ball. Knot threads. Flatten snout slightly. Glue then slip-stitch in place on face.

9. **Face:** With dark brown yarn, embroider nose and smiling mouth as shown in photo. Appliqué black eye circles on larger brown eye circles. With white thread, embroider two small stitches for highlight on each eye. Glue then slipstitch eyes in place on either side of snout.

10. Comb all seams so they are concealed by fur pile.

Yum Yum

DESIGN BY ANNA HOBBS

He looks like a cute cookie, but this gingerbread man is made of felt. Simply cut him out, stitch on the jumbo rickrack to look like icing, and then glue on his face and buttons. Once you've stitched his front and back together, he's ready for stuffing.

Finished gingerbread man stands 24 1/2 in. (62.0 cm) tall.

YOU NEED

- **5/8 yd. (0.50 m) brown felt, 72 in. (180.0 cm) wide**
- **Scraps of colored felt for eyes, nose, mouth and buttons**
- **3 1/4 yd. (3.00 m) jumbo white rickrack**
- **1 yd. (0.90 m) red ribbon, 7/8 in. (2.3 cm) wide**
- **Polyester fiberfill**
- **White craft glue**
- **Brown paper**

To enlarge pattern, see General Directions (page 130).

1. Cut two gingerbread men from brown felt.

2. Starting and ending at crotch, machine-stitch rickrack 1 in. (2.5 cm) in from edge of front. Cut eyes, nose, mouth and buttons from felt scraps. Glue in place.

3. With wrong sides together, edgestitch front to back, leaving open between notches. Stuff. Stitch opening closed. Tie ribbon around neck.

YUM YUM

leave open

FRONT & BACK
cut 2
brown felt

Henderson Bear

DESIGN BY HELEN HENDERSON

For the teddy bear lover in all of us, here is a lovable, huggable and movable teddy perfect for Christmas gift-giving. Joint discs inserted in the neck and at the shoulders and hips mean Henderson Bear can sit, "walk" and most of all, hug you right back.

Finished bear is approx. 15 3/4 in. (40.0 cm) tall.

YOU NEED

- **5/8 yd. (0.50 m) camel-colored fake fur with 3/8 in. (1.0 cm) pile, 60 in. (approx. 150.0 cm) wide**
- **Piece of imitation suede, 6 in. (15.0 cm) square**
- **Brown embroidery thread**
- **Matching thread**
- **Buttonhole twist thread**

- **Two brown lock-in eyes, 5/8 in. (1.5 cm) in diameter**
- **Four doll joints, 1 1/8 in. (3.0 cm) in diameter**
- **One doll joint, 1 3/4 in. (4.5 cm) in diameter**
- **Embroidery needle**
- **Polyester fiberfill**
- **Water-soluble fabric marker**
- **Brown paper**

Note: Use a 1/4 in. (0.6 cm) seam allowance throughout, unless otherwise indicated. Backstitch at beginning and end of seams.

For pattern pieces, see page 139. To enlarge pattern, see General Directions (page 130).

1. From imitation suede, cut two paws (reversing one) and two soles.

2. Place remaining pattern pieces on wrong side of single thickness of fake fur, positioning each piece so arrow runs in direction of nap. To determine direction of nap, stroke fur in whichever direction will make it lie flat and feel smoothest. Trace around pattern pieces with marker, being careful to reverse pattern pieces for body, arms, legs and sides. Transfer all pattern markings. Cut out pieces. Use tip of scissors only to snip through fabric backing, being careful not to cut fur on right side.

3. Stitch darts on each head side. With right sides together, stitch head sides together from A to B. With right sides together, pin head crest to head sides matching points A and C on each piece. Stitch around head crest from C to A to C on opposite side. Clip curves. Turn head right-side out. Cut small eye holes in face as indicated. Insert eye shanks. Lock in place on wrong side.

4. Stuff head firmly. With buttonhole twist, run a gathering thread around neck opening. Insert 1 3/4 in. (4.5 cm) joint disc with post into neck opening. Pull gathers tight around disc, allowing post to stick out of neck opening. Tie thread securely.

5. With right sides together, stitch two ear pieces, leaving open where indicated. Clip curves. Turn right-side out. Topstitch ear opening closed. Trim close to topstitching. Repeat for second ear. Pin ears to head at positions indicated. Using buttonhole twist, slipstitch ears securely in place.

6. With brown floss and using satin stitch, embroider nose and mouth.

7. Pierce very small holes in both body pieces for arm and leg joints.

8. With right sides of body pieces together, stitch from D to E and from F to G. With buttonhole twist, run a gathering thread around neck opening. Pull gathers tight and tie threads securely. Turn body right-side out.

9. Position head on top of body, pushing post from head disc through hole in neck gathers of body. Slip washer onto post, then push locking washer up post as far as it will go. Joint must be tight.

10. With right sides together and straight edges even,

stitch suede paw to inner arm. Pierce small hole in inner arm for arm joint. With right sides together, stitch outer arm to inner arm, leaving open at top where indicated. Clip curves. Turn right-side out. Stuff arm firmly to joint hole. Repeat for second arm.

11. Making sure that arms are on correct side of body and are facing forward, insert 1 1/8 in. (3.0 cm) joint disc with post from inside of each arm through hole in arm and corresponding hole in body. On inside of body, slip washers onto posts and then push locking washers up posts as far as possible.

12. Finish stuffing arms and slipstitch openings closed.

13. With right sides of two legs together, stitch from H to J and from K to L. Clip corner and curves. With right sides together and notches matching seam lines, stitch suede sole to bottom of foot. Pierce a small hole on inside of leg for joint. Stuff leg firmly up to joint hole. Repeat for second leg, making sure to pierce hole in opposite inner leg so you will have a left and right leg.

14. Attach legs to body as given for arms in Step 11.

15. Finish stuffing legs and slipstitch openings closed.

16. Stuff body firmly, putting lots of stuffing around joints to pad them. Slipstitch opening G–E closed.

17. Comb all seams so they are concealed by fur pile.

Merry Mary

DESIGN BY DENISE FLYS

Make a child's Christmas dream come true with the gift of a precious doll. Merry Mary is fun to sew. Included are patterns for her nightgown, dust cap and boots. She's definitely a cuddly charmer.

Finished doll is approx. 22 in. (56.0 cm) tall.

YOU NEED

FOR BODY:

- **3/4 yd. (0.60 m) flesh-tone broadcloth, 45 in. (approx. 115.0 cm) wide**
- **One ball (25 g) dark brown mohair yarn, for hair**
- **Scrap of brown felt, for eyes**
- **Brown thread, for mouth**

- **Polyester fiberfill**

FOR CLOTHES:

- **1 5/8 yd. (1.50 m) flannelette, 45 in. (115.0 cm) wide**
- **1 1/8 yd. (1.00 m) satin ribbon, 3/8 in. (1.0 cm) wide**
- **1 1/8 yd. (1.00 m) lingerie elastic**
- **Two snap fasteners**

Note: Sew fabric with right sides together, using a 1/4 in. (0.6 cm) seam allowance throughout.

For pattern pieces, see page 139. To enlarge pattern, see General Directions (page 130).

BODY

1. From flesh-tone broadcloth, cut body front, two body backs, four arms and four legs.

2. **Arms:** With right sides together, stitch two arm pieces together, leaving open at top. Turn right-side out. Stuff hand only enough to give a little thickness to fingers. Topstitch along finger lines as shown on pattern. Continue stuffing to broken line (elbow). Topstitch along this line. This makes the arm flexible. Stuff upper arm and machine-stitch closed. Repeat for second arm.

3. **Legs:** With right sides together, stitch two leg pieces together, leaving open at top. Turn right-side out. Stuff to broken line (knee). Fold leg so front and back seams align. Topstitch along knee line. This makes the leg flexible. Stuff upper leg and machine-stitch closed. Repeat for second leg.

4. **Body:** With right sides together, stitch body back pieces together along center back seam. Stitch body front to body back around head from point A on one side to point A on opposite side. Reinforce stitching at corners. Clip. Insert arms between front and back pieces (right sides still together) so top of each arm is even with raw edge of side seam between A and B and so hands point down toward center of body. Stitch side seams, catching arms in stitching. Turn body right-side out. With right sides together and raw edges even, stitch top of legs to bottom edge of body back, making sure feet will point forward. Stuff head and body firmly. Slipstitch bottom opening closed.

5. **Hair:** Cut twenty-seven strands of yarn, each 35 1/2 in. (approx. 90.0 cm) long. Tie bundle of yarn in middle and sew securely to doll's forehead at X shown on pattern. Smooth over each side of head, framing face. Gather together hair about halfway down each side of head and sew to large dots indicated on pattern. Braid remainder of strands and tie at ends. Cut a piece of cardboard 14 in. (35.0 cm) long. Wind yarn around it fifty-five times. Do not cut. Before removing from card, tie loops together through center of bundle. Sew this point to top of head, just behind hair already in place. Smooth evenly around back and sides of head. Tack ends of loops in place along back of neck to look like curls.

6. **Face:** Cut small circles of brown felt for eyes. Sew in place. Embroider a smile with a single strand of brown thread.

DUST CAP

1. With right sides together, stitch cap pieces together, leaving a 2 3/4 in. (7.0 cm) opening where indicated. Turn right side out. Press.

2. To form casing, topstitch 2 in. (5.0 cm) from outer edge. Topstitch 3/8 in. (1.0 cm) outside this line, leaving a small opening at same point where seam has been left

open. Insert elastic through these openings and through casing. Pull up to fit doll's head and sew ends of elastic together. Topstitch casing opening closed. Slipstitch seam opening closed.

3. Tie a small ribbon bow and attach to front of cap.

NIGHTGOWN

1. From flannelette, cut nightgown front (on fold), two backs, two sleeves, two yoke fronts, two right back yokes, two left back yokes, one strip 20 x 3 in. (51.0 x 7.5 cm) for neck ruffle, one strip 38 x 2 in. (96.0 x 5.0 cm) for yoke ruffle and two strips each 38 x 5 in. (96.0 x 12.5 cm) for hem ruffle. Also cut two dust cap and four boot pieces.

2. Stitch front and back yokes together at shoulders. Repeat with remaining yoke pieces for yoke facing.

3. Fold neck ruffle in half so right sides are together and long edges meet. Stitch ends. Turn right-side out. Press. Run a line of gathering stitches down raw edge, 1/4 in. (0.6 cm) from edge. Pull up thread and pin ruffle to neck edge of yoke between C and C, adjusting gathers to fit. Baste.

4. Narrowly hem one long edge and both ends of yoke ruffle. Gather raw edge, and with right sides together, pin to lower edge of yoke between D and D, adjusting gathers to fit. Baste.

5. With right sides together, stitch yoke facing to yoke down center back edges and around neck. Turn right-side out. Press.

6. Stitch back pieces together from bottom edge to E. Turn under and hem center back opening edges.

7. Stitch sleeves to front and back of nightgown at raglan seams. Gather top edge of front/back, and with right sides together, pin around lower edge of yoke (do not pin to facing), matching center of sleeve to yoke shoulder seam and adjusting gathers evenly to fit. Stitch. Turn under lower edge of yoke facing and slip-stitch in place. Sew snap fasteners to right and left back yoke edges.

8. Turn under 1/4 in. (0.6 cm), then 1 1/8 in. (3.0 cm), along bottom of each sleeve. Topstitch close to first fold, then 3/8 in. (1.0 cm) from this to form casing. Insert elastic and secure at one end of casing. Pull up to fit

around doll's wrist and secure at other end of casing. Thread elastic through other sleeve in same manner. Stitch sleeve and side seams.

9. Stitch short ends of two hem ruffle strips together to form a loop. Narrowly hem both edges. Gather 3/4 in. (2.0 cm) from one edge. Lap gathered edge of ruffle 1 in. (2.5 cm) over bottom edge of nightgown. Pin in place, adjusting gathers to fit. Topstitch along gathering line.

10. Tie a small ribbon bow and attach to front neck.

BOOTS

1. With right sides together, stitch two boot pieces together from F to G.

2. Turn under 1/4 in. (0.6 cm) then 3/8 in. (1.0 cm) around top of boot. Topstitch close to first fold. Insert elastic through casing. Pull up to fit doll's ankle and secure at both ends. Make second boot in same manner.

3. Stitch remaining section of center back seams closed.

CHAPTER 7

Gifts to Make

Hostess Gifts

During the holiday season or any time of the year, delight your favorite host or hostess with a thoughtful, handmade gift. It's one of the most individual ways to say "thank you."

Scented Fire Starters

YOU NEED

- Christmas paper baking cups
- Oil of cinnamon (available at drugstores and specialty food shops)
- Sawdust
- Paraffin wax or old candles

1. Line muffin tins with paper baking cups. Fill each three-quarters full with sawdust. Add a drop of oil of cinnamon to each.

2. Melt paraffin wax or old candles in top of double boiler. Allow approx. 1/4 cup (50 mL) of wax per muffin tin. Pour over sawdust. Let stand.

3. When cool and hardened, starters are ready for use. Package as desired with instructions to place two or three beneath kindling and logs in the fireplace.

Bird Feeder

YOU NEED

- Small cedar, fir or hard wood tree branch, 4 in. (10.0 cm) diameter, approx. 12 in. (30.0 cm) long
- 1/4 in. (0.6 cm) dowelling, 36 in. (91.5 cm) long
- 1/4 in. screw eye, approx. 3 in. (7.5 cm) long
- Electric drill with 1/4 in. (6.35 mm) and 1 in. (25.5 mm) bits
- Wood glue
- 10 in. (25.5 cm) thick plastic-covered wire
- Bird food and suet

1. Drill twelve to twenty 1 in. (25.4 mm) holes, 1 in. (2.5 cm) deep, spaced at random around the branch. Drill a 1/4 in. (6.35 mm) hole, 1/4 in. (0.6 cm) deep, 1 in. below each large hole.

2. Cut dowelling into 2 1/2 in. (6.0 cm) long pieces. Glue these into small holes. Insert screw eye into top of branch. Loop wire through eye to hang.

3. Mix bird food with suet and pack into large holes.

Luxurious Gifts

DESIGNS BY CAROLYN SMITH

A lot of luxury for a little price... With a bit of time and imagination, you can turn fine fabrics and flea-market finds into exquisite, one-of-a-kind, handmade presents. Rich-looking velvet added to an antique napkin ring becomes an elegant Pincushion or Earring Holder. Vintage coins, buttons and beads can be worked into unique Cufflinks, Stickpins and Necklaces. A suede Jewelry Box can store these treasures. Marbleized Gift Boxes and Packets make lovely packages for handmade gifts. All are elegant ways to say "I care."

Pincushion

YOU NEED	
• Piece of purple velvet, 6 in. (15.0 cm) square	• Heavy thread
• Piece of black felt, 2 in. (5.0 cm) square	• Polyester fiberfill
• Napkin ring	• White craft glue
• Piece of lightweight cardboard, 2 in. (5.0 cm) square	• Geometry compass
	• Dressmaker's chalk

1. Using compass, draw a 5 1/8 in. (13.0 cm) diameter circle on wrong side of velvet. Cut out. Run a line of gathering stitches around edge of circle. Place a handful of fiberfill on wrong side. Pull up gathering thread, adjusting stuffing to form a ball (ball should be slightly larger in diameter than napkin ring). Check size and firmness of ball by pushing into ring. Adjust if necessary. Knot thread.

2. Apply glue to inside of ring. Push ball into ring, smooth side up. Let dry.

3. Trace around ring onto cardboard. Cut out. Trim circle to fit into bottom of ring. Glue around edge of circle and insert into bottom of ring.

4. Trace around ring onto felt. Cut out. Glue felt circle to cardboard at bottom of ring.

Earring Holder

YOU NEED	
• Piece of purple velvet, 7 x 4 in. (18.0 x 10.0 cm) square	• Lightweight cardboard
• Piece of black felt, 2 in. (5.0 cm) square	• White craft glue
• Napkin ring	• Dressmaker's chalk

1. Trace around napkin ring onto cardboard. Cut out. Trim circle to fit into bottom of ring. Trace around ring onto wrong side of velvet. Draw a line 3/4 in. (2.0 cm) outside traced line (for folding allowance). Cut out. Center and glue cardboard circle to wrong side of velvet circle. Cut several notches in folding allowance and fold around cardboard. Glue in place. Glue around edge of covered circle and insert into bottom of ring so right side faces up inside the ring.

2. Trace around ring onto felt. Cut out. Glue felt circle to covered cardboard at bottom of ring.

3. Measure inside depth of napkin ring. Cut a cardboard strip approx. 8 in. (20.0 cm) long x depth. Fit strip around inside of ring and trim so ends are 1/8 in. (0.3 cm) short of meeting. Trace around cardboard strip onto wrong side of velvet. Draw lines 3/8 in. (1.0 cm) outside traced lines (for folding allowance). Cut out. Center and glue cardboard strip to wrong side of velvet strip. Cut notches in folding allowance at each corner and fold around cardboard. Glue in place. Apply glue to inside of ring. Fit covered strip around inside of ring. Let dry.

Bead Necklace

YOU NEED	
• **Assorted beads and pendants (purchased or from old jewelry)**	• **Tiger tail wire (nylon-covered beading wire) or nylon fishing line**
• **Necklace clasp**	• **Pliers**

1. Cover work area with cloth or towel to prevent beads from rolling.

2. Cut a length of beading wire slightly longer than desired length of finished necklace. Thread beads, starting arrangement at center and working out to both ends.

3. Tie one half of clasp securely to each end as close as possible to last bead.

Jewelry Box

Note: When gluing suede, sponge off any excess glue immediately with warm water.

YOU NEED

- **3/8 yd. (0.30 m) synthetic suede, 45 in. (approx. 115.0 cm) wide**
- **3/8 yd. (0.30 m) compressed polyester batting (such as Thermolam), 45 in. wide**
- **Piece of lightweight cardboard, 21 x 9 in. (53.0 x 23.0 cm)**
- **Decoration for lid, such as an old brooch, insignia, initial or blazer crest**
- **Matching thread**
- **White craft glue**
- **Zipper foot**
- **Brown paper**

Draw and cut pattern from brown paper, following measurements on Diagram (page 122).

1. From suede, cut two box pieces using paper pattern and three lid rectangles as follows: A, 9 x 7 1/4 in. (23.0 x 18.5 cm); B, 7 x 4 3/4 in. (18.0 x 12.0 cm); C, 7 x 5 in. (18.0 x 12.5 cm). With right sides together and using a 1/4 in. (0.6 cm) seam allowance, stitch two box pieces together around all edges, leaving open between large dots. Turn right-side out.

2. Cut two cardboard rectangles and four batting rectangles in each of the following sizes: 6 1/4 x 1 5/8 in. (16.0 x 4.0 cm), for front and back; 4 1/2 x 1 5/8 in. (11.5 x 4.0 cm), for sides. Cut one cardboard and two batting rectangles 6 1/4 x 4 1/2 in. (16.0 x 11.5 cm), for bottom. (You should have a total of five cardboard and ten batting rectangles.)

3. Glue a cardboard rectangle between two corresponding batting rectangles. Let dry. Insert rectangles into suede to check for proper fit. There should be a narrow gap between the rectangles to allow for folding. Remove rectangles to trim, if necessary.

4. Firmly push front rectangle into suede. Using zipper foot, stitch along fold line, through both layers. Repeat for sides, bottom and back. Turn under 1/4 in. (0.6 cm) around opening and slipstitch closed.

5. Fold up sides, front and back as indicated by curved arrows. Glue inside edge of corners together. Glue one corner at a time, holding in place with straight pins until glue dries.

6. **Lid:** Cut one cardboard rectangle and two batting rectangles 7 1/4 x 5 3/8 in. (18.5 x 13.5 cm). Glue cardboard rectangle between two batting rectangles. Center and glue to wrong side of suede lid rectangle A.

Fold under and glue edges of suede to wrong side, mitring at corners. Center and glue rectangle B to wrong side, covering cardboard. Cut a 6 1/8 x 4 in. (15.5 x 10.0 cm) cardboard rectangle. Center and glue to wrong side of C. Fold under and glue edges of suede to wrong side, mitring at corners. Center and glue to wrong side of larger covered lid.

7. Glue decoration to center front of box lid.

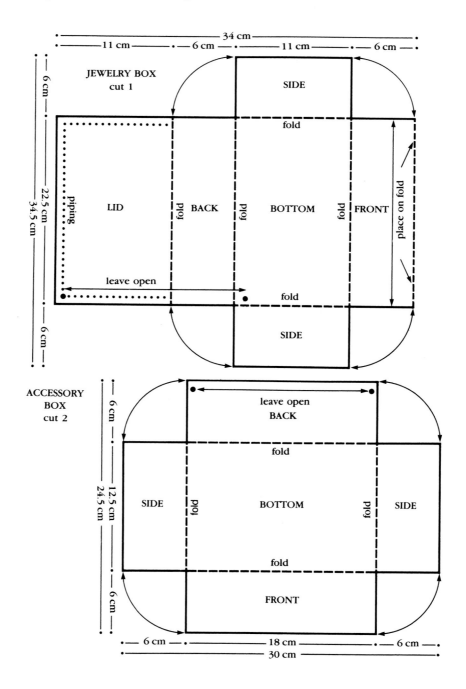

Marbleized Gift Boxes and Tags

YOU NEED

- **Small shaker boxes**
- **Lightweight cardboard or Bristol board for gift boxes and tags**
- **Gold spray paint**
- **Small amounts of oil-based paint**
- **Coordinating ribbon**
- **Gold cord**
- **Pan (such as an old plastic dishpan)**
- **Newspaper**
- **Stir stick**
- **Utility knife**
- **Hole punch**
- **White craft glue**
- **Brown paper**

TO MARBLEIZE ITEMS:

Cover work area with newspaper. Fill pan with water. Pour in a few drops of oil-based paints and stir gently. Paint swirls will float on the surface. To transfer swirling pattern onto something flat, such as paper or ribbon, place on surface of water and lift off. To transfer onto something that has more depth, grip inside of article with splayed fingers and immerse it in water up to the top edge and lift out. Use a slow, steady down-and-up motion. Place right-side up on newspaper. Let dry.

MARBLEIZED BOX

1. Spray-paint box and lid, inside and out. Let dry.

2. Fill pan with water, 1 in. (2.5 cm) deeper than height of box. Add paint and stir. Immerse box. Lift out and place upside down on newspaper to dry. Repeat for lid.

3. Tie lid to box with cord or marbleized ribbon.

GIFT PACKET AND TAG

Draw and cut pattern for gift tag and/or box from brown paper, following measurements on Diagrams (at left).

1. Cut box or tag from cardboard. Spray-paint both sides. Let dry.

2. Fill pan with water, add paint and stir. Place one side of cardboard on surface of water. Lift off and let dry, marbleized-side up.

3. Score fold lines with scissor blade. Cut slit and punch hole in gift tag. Fold up with marbleized-side out. Poke pointed tab into slit to close. Tie loop of cord through hole. Fold gift box in half. Dab glue along narrow flap and glue to inside of box. Fold curved ends in. Tie closed with cord or marbleized ribbon.

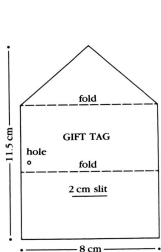

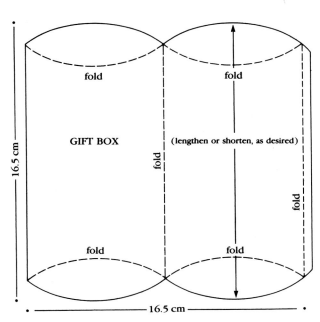

GIFT BOX

16.5 cm

fold · fold · fold · fold · fold · fold

(lengthen or shorten, as desired)

16.5 cm

GIFT TAG

hole · fold · fold

11.5 cm

2 cm slit

8 cm

Elegant Evening Bag

DESIGN BY BEVERLEY McINNES

For that special friend or relative on your Christmas list, create a gift she will treasure. Stitched in shades of blue accented with rose and gold and decorated with a gold tassel, it's an unusual little purse to be carried and cherished season after season.

YOU NEED

- **No. 13 ecru mono canvas, two pieces 9 in. (23.0 cm) square**
- **Piece of lining fabric such as taffeta or medium-weight silky fabric, 18 1/2 x 9 in. (46.0 x 23.0 cm)**
- **Matching thread**
- **Two skeins each of DMC embroidery floss in shades of blue, No. 791, No. 792, No. 793, No. 794**
- **One skein each of Marlitt viscose embroidery floss, No. 209 deep rose and No. 019 light rose**

- **12 yd. (11.00 m) DMC Fil Or (gold)**
- **No. 22 tapestry needle**
- **Stretcher frame, 9 in. (23.0 cm) square (optional)**
- **Masking tape**
- **Metal ring, 2 in. (5.0 cm) in diameter**
- **8 in. (20.0 cm) gold chain**
- **Gold tassel**

1. Bind edges of canvas pieces with masking tape and staple to frame, if using one.

2. Following graph, work repetitive design over an area 6 3/4 in. (17.0 cm) long x 5 1/4 in. (13.5 cm) wide as follows: First work encroached cross-stitch Xs with all 6 plies of DMC floss (separate plies before threading needle). Work compensating stitches at beginning and end of rows where necessary. Alternate color of pattern repeat, working with four shades of blue (e.g., repeat dark to light sequence or work dark to light to dark again, creating a mirror image of colors). Lay horizontal threads of Marlitt viscose floss across Xs over width of work, alternating 8 threads of one color then 8 threads of the other. Couch these threads down with Fil Or, where indicated.

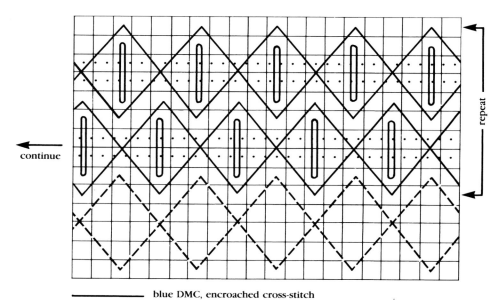

continue →

repeat

———————— blue DMC, encroached cross-stitch

· · · · · · · rose Marlitt, tramé

DMC Fil Or, couched

Using 5 plies of DMC floss, work 2 rows of continental stitch around edges of entire design. Work second needlepoint panel in same manner.

3. Trim edges of unworked canvas to within 3/4 in. (2.0 cm) of stitched work. Press under all edges of canvas, mitring at corners and leaving 2 rows of mesh along each edge for finishing stitches.

4. Cut two rectangles of lining fabric, 5/8 in. (1.5 cm) larger than size of pressed needlepoint panels. Press under 5/8 in. on all edges of each piece. Using tiny stitches, slipstitch lining to back of each needlepoint panel, wrong sides together. Be sure the lining does not extend beyond the unworked rows of mesh around edges of panel.

5. Using 4 plies of DMC floss, work herringbone or binding stitch along top edge of each panel. Place front and back panels wrong sides together. Join the panels and finish edges by working binding stitch around sides and bottom.

6. Loop chain through metal ring. With pliers, open link at one end of chain and join to link at other end, forming a complete circle. Sew tassel and one link of chain to side edge of purse approx 2 in. (5.0 cm) from top. To close bag, pleat top edge and push through metal ring.

Wild Rose Wood Carving

DESIGNS BY JO CALVERT

Hand-carving is a time-honored tradition that can turn the most practical items into gifts of beauty. The carved motif in this breadboard and shelf is a stylized Canadian wild rose, found in fields from Quebec to the Yukon in summertime.

YOU NEED

FOR BOTH PROJECTS:

- X-ACTO knife or utility knife
- Two carving tools approx. 1/8 in. (0.3 cm) deep, one a sharp V-shape and the other a shallow crescent shape
- Soft pencil
- Fine sandpaper
- Tracing paper

FOR BREADBOARD:

- Hardwood breadboard
- Mineral oil and rag

For shelf:

- 3 ft. (0.91 m) length of 1 x 6 in. (2.5 x 15.0 cm) hardwood
- Two 2 in. (5.0 cm) wood screws
- Two 1 in. (2.5 cm) wood screws
- Drill with bits to correspond to screws
- Jigsaw
- Clamps
- Screwdriver
- Carpenter's glue
- Varnish or wax
- Brown paper

BREADBOARD

TO TRANSFER DESIGN (shown actual size on page 134):

Trace solid lines of wild rose motif onto tracing paper with soft pencil. Turn paper over. Retrace lines on reverse side. Place paper right-side up on right side of board, keeping design at least 5/8 in. (1.5 cm) from edges of board. Firmly redraw over lines of design, using just enough pressure to transfer lines onto wood.

TO CARVE:

Note: Be sure to carve away from yourself, turning board when necessary. Work slowly, rocking blade slightly as you carve. To prevent chipped edges, always carve towards a cut edge. Carved areas should slope towards center of design. If carving becomes deeper than depth of vertical cuts along outlines, recut outlines with knife to preserve a clean edge.

1. With knife, make a vertical cut at least 1/8 in. (0.3 cm) deep along all solid lines of design. These cuts act as a guide for the carving tools and prevent the blade from slipping.

2. Using V tool, carve along all cut lines. Using crescent tool, carve out all areas of petals indicated by dots. Carve towards center of flower, stopping at cut line. Also with crescent tool, carve out interior of each leaf indicated by dots, stopping at cut line around edge of petals. Using V tool, carve a vein line on each leaf. Finally, using crescent tool and carving towards center, carve around all edges of flower and leaves where indicated by dots.

3. Using V tool, carve a line around inside edge of breadboard.

4. Sand finished board and carved areas lightly. Rub with mineral oil (do not use furniture oil, as this can be toxic).

SHELF
To enlarge diagram/pattern, see General Directions (page 130).

1. Trace outline of shelf, brace and two supports onto wood following diagram layout. Cut out.

2. Drill holes to fit long screws 1 1/4 in. (3.2 cm) in from each end of front surface of brace. Having back edges flush, fit top surface of brace against underside of shelf as indicated by broken lines on Diagram. From underside of brace, drill 1 in. (25.4 mm) deep holes (through brace and part way into shelf) to fit shorter screws, 2 in. (5.0 cm) in from each end.

3. Positioning motif as shown, transfer wild rose motif onto one side of one shelf support as given in Breadboard instructions. Turn tracing paper over and transfer reversed design onto opposite side of other shelf support (each support should be a mirror image of the other).

4. Carve designs as for Breadboard, Steps 1 to 3.

5. Round and sand edges of shelf and shelf support. Sand carved areas lightly.

6. Glue and screw brace to underside of shelf. Having back and front edges flush and carved designs facing outward, glue top edge of shelf supports to underside of shelf where indicated by broken lines. Clamp. Let dry.

7. Lightly sand assembled shelf. Wax or varnish as desired. Attach shelf to wall with two long screws.

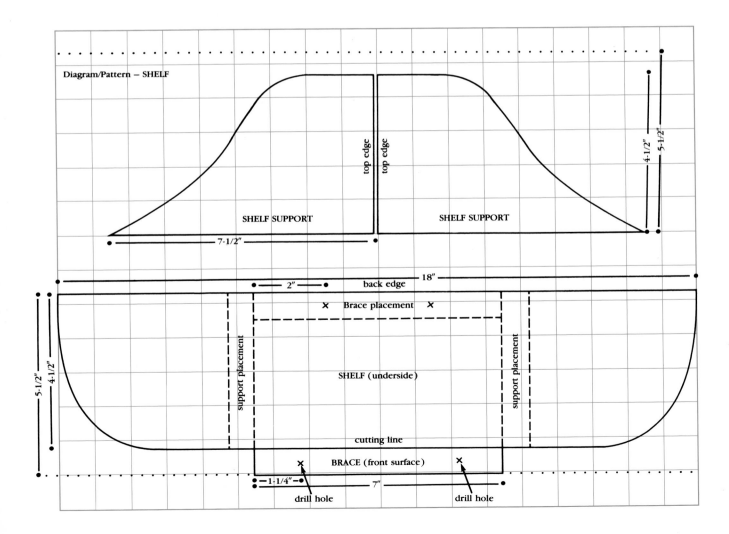

Diagram/Pattern – SHELF

Trompe l'Oeil Window

DESIGN BY JANE BUCKLES

Some gifts can't be bought at any price — especially ones handcrafted with a special person in mind. For the executive in a windowless office, make a Trompe l'Oeil Window, and turn his or her workspace into a unique room with a view.

YOU NEED

- **Piece of 3/8 in. (1.0 cm) plywood, good on one side, 21 1/2 x 30 3/4 in. (54.6 x 76.8 cm)**
- **Piece of 1 x 4 in.* (2.5 x 10.0 cm) pine, 90 in. (2.29 m) long**
- **Piece of 1 x 5 in.* (2.5 x 12.5 cm) pine, 45 in. (1.14 m) long**
- **Scraps of 1 in. (2.5 cm) pine, approx 14 x 7 in. (35.0 x 18.0 cm), for pot and tulips**
- **Strip of cove or quarter-round molding, 22 in. (56.0 cm) long**
- **3/8 in. (1.0 cm) dowelling, 15 in. (38.0 cm) long**
- **Drill with 3/8 in. (9.525 mm) bit and bit to correspond to size of screws**
- **1 in. (2.5 cm) screws**

- **1 1/4 in. (3.2 cm) spiral finishing nails**
- **Two screw eyes**
- **Picture frame wire**
- **Hammer**
- **Saw**
- **Jigsaw**
- **X-ACTO knife**
- **Sandpaper**
- **White craft glue**
- **White primer paint**
- **Acrylic or oil-based paint, colors as desired**
- **Paintbrushes**
- **Brown paper**

*These measurements are nominal sizes quoted by lumber industry. Actual size is generally 1/2 to 3/4 in. less.

To enlarge window scene and flowerpot patterns, see General Directions (page 130).

1. From 1 x 4 in. (2.5 x 10.0 cm) pine, cut two pieces each 22 1/2 in. (57.2 cm) long and one piece 22 in. (60.0 cm) long for window frame. From 1 x 5 in. (2.5 x 12.5 cm) pine, cut one piece 22 in. long and another piece 23 in. (58.4 cm) long for windowsill. Lightly sand these pieces as well as plywood rectangle and molding.

2. Paint molding, frame and sill pieces in desired color. Paint good side of plywood with primer. Let dry. Transfer enlarged outdoor scene or draw your own scene on primed plywood. Paint as desired or use photo as a guide. Paint or stencil small details such as sheep in foreground, blind pull and snowflakes.

3. Trace pattern for flowerpot and two tulips onto scraps of 1 in. (2.5 cm) pine. Cut out with a jigsaw. From

dowelling, cut stems 6 1/2 in. (16.5 cm) long and 5 in. (12.5 cm) long, and two 1 1/4 in. (3.2 cm) dowel pins. Paint flowerpot, tulips and stems. Let dry.

Drill a 3/8 in. (9.525 mm) hole in bottom of each flower. Glue and insert stems. Drill similar holes in top of flowerpot, approx 3 in. (7.5 cm) apart. Glue and insert stems.

4. Drill two 3/8 in. (9.525 mm) holes in bottom of flowerpot. Glue and insert dowel pins.

5. Center and nail 23 in. (58.4 cm) length of 1 x 5 in. (2.5 x 12.5 cm) pine at right angles to and onto top edge of 22 in. (56.0 cm) piece to form windowsill (see Diagram).

6. Referring to Diagram, assemble remaining pieces to form a frame around painted side of plywood, so frame overlaps approx 1/4 in. (0.6 cm) over edge of plywood. Screw pieces securely in place from back of window. Glue molding in place under sill.

7. Drill two 3/8 in. (9.525 mm) holes in windowsill to take dowel pins on bottom of flowerpot. Insert flowerpot. Do not glue. Wooden pot may be replaced by a real pot of flowers when desired.

8. Insert screw eyes into either side of back of window. String picture wire between two eyes to hang.

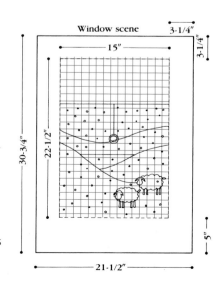

Window scene

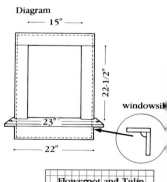

Diagram

windowsill

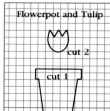

Flowerpot and Tulip

General Directions

To Enlarge Patterns

Enlarge pattern by the squaring method, as follows: On brown paper, draw a grid of horizontal and vertical lines 1 in. (2.5 cm) apart. Each square on the diagram equals a 1 in. square on your paper. Enlarge by drawing each line of the design onto the corresponding square on your paper. Transfer any markings.

To Transfer Patterns

There are several methods of transferring a pattern. Choose the one best suited to the pattern and materials used.

Carbon paper or dressmaker's carbon

Use carbon paper for paper and cardboard projects only. Use dressmaker's carbon for fabric, in a color close to that of the fabric. Place carbon face down on fabric. Place pattern on top. With tracing wheel or pencil, draw over pattern, using just enough pressure to transfer lines.

Soft pencil

Use on wood or cardboard. Using soft pencil, trace pattern onto tracing paper. Turn paper over. Retrace lines on reverse side. Place paper right-side up on wood or cardboard. Firmly redraw pattern, using just enough pressure to transfer lines.

Basting

To transfer pattern to dark, soft, heavily textured, stretchy or sheer fabrics, trace pattern onto tissue paper. Pin to fabric. Hand- or machine-baste around lines. Tear away tissue. When work is complete, remove basting.

Water-soluble marking pen

Use on needlepoint canvas and sheer, washable fabrics. With pattern under canvas or fabric, lightly trace design onto right side. To remove markings, dampen fabric, and drawn lines will disappear.

Knitting and Crochet Abbreviations

beg = begin(ning)
CC = contrasting color
ch = chain
cm = centimeter(s)
dc = double crochet
dec = decrease(s) (d) (ing)
g = gram(s)
inc = increase(s) (d) (ing)
in(s) = inch(es)
k = knit
lp(s) = loop(s)
M1 = make 1 stitch by picking up horizontal loop in front of next stitch and knitting into back of it
MC = main color
mm = millimeter(s)
p = purl
psso = pass slip stitch(es) over
rem = remain(ing)
rep = repeat(ed) (ing)
rnd(s) = round(s)
sc = single crochet
sk = skip
sl = slip
sl st = slip stitch
sp(s) = space(s)
st(s) = stitch(es)
St st = stocking stitch
tbl = through back of loop
tog = together

Simplified Instructions

All knitting and crochet instructions that appear in this book conform to national knitting and crochet standards.

Tension

It is essential to work to the exact tension with the specified yarn to obtain satisfactory results. Before beginning any knitting or crochet project, make a test swatch at least 4 in. (approx. 10.0 cm) square using the specified yarn, needles or hook and stitch pattern. Individual knitting and crochet tension may vary, so it may be necessary to adjust needle or hook size to achieve the tension given. TO SAVE TIME, TAKE TIME TO CHECK TENSION.

Full-Size Patterns

The full-size patterns appearing on the following pages can be traced or photocopied for use with the corresponding instructions found in the main body of this book.

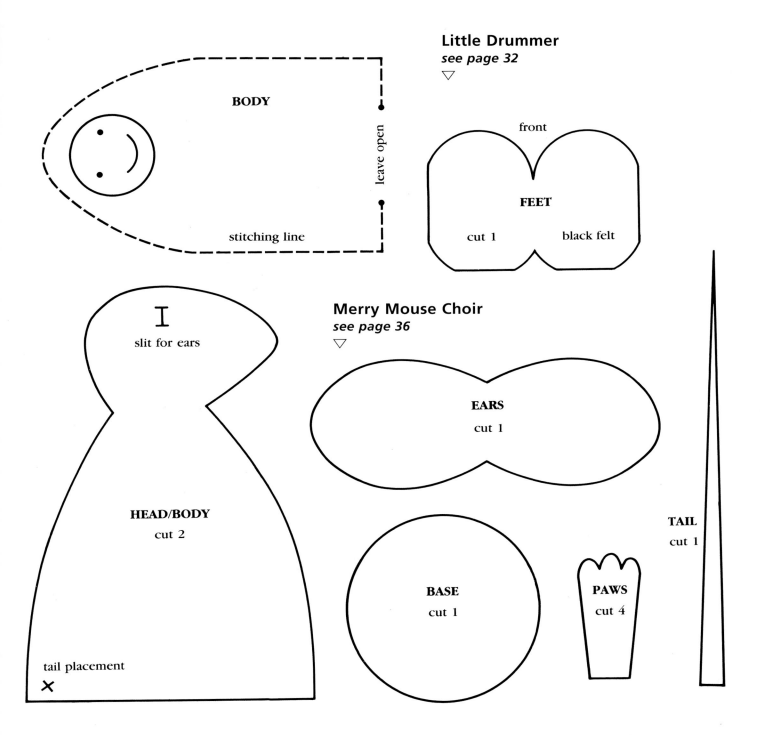

Little Drummer
see page 32
▽

BODY

leave open

stitching line

front

FEET

cut 1   black felt

Merry Mouse Choir
see page 36
▽

slit for ears

EARS

cut 1

HEAD/BODY

cut 2

TAIL

cut 1

BASE

cut 1

PAWS

cut 4

tail placement

✗

Full-Size Patterns

Cheeky Little Angel
see page 46
▷

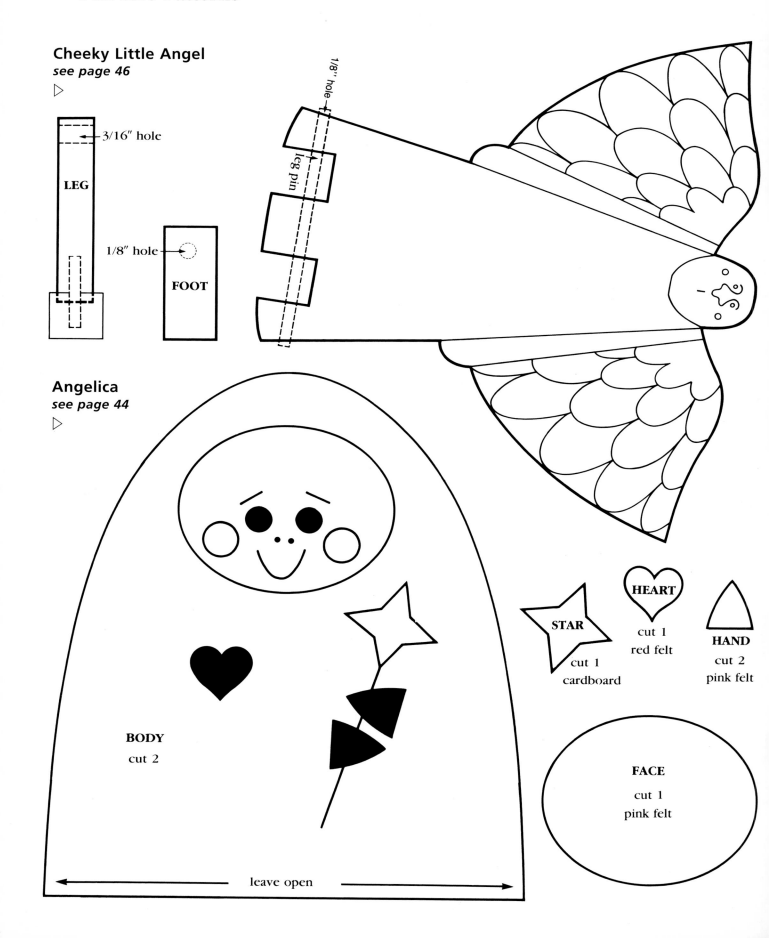

3/16" hole

LEG

1/8" hole

FOOT

1/8" hole

leg pin

Angelica
see page 44
▷

BODY

cut 2

leave open

STAR

cut 1
cardboard

HEART

cut 1
red felt

HAND

cut 2
pink felt

FACE

cut 1
pink felt

Full-Size Patterns

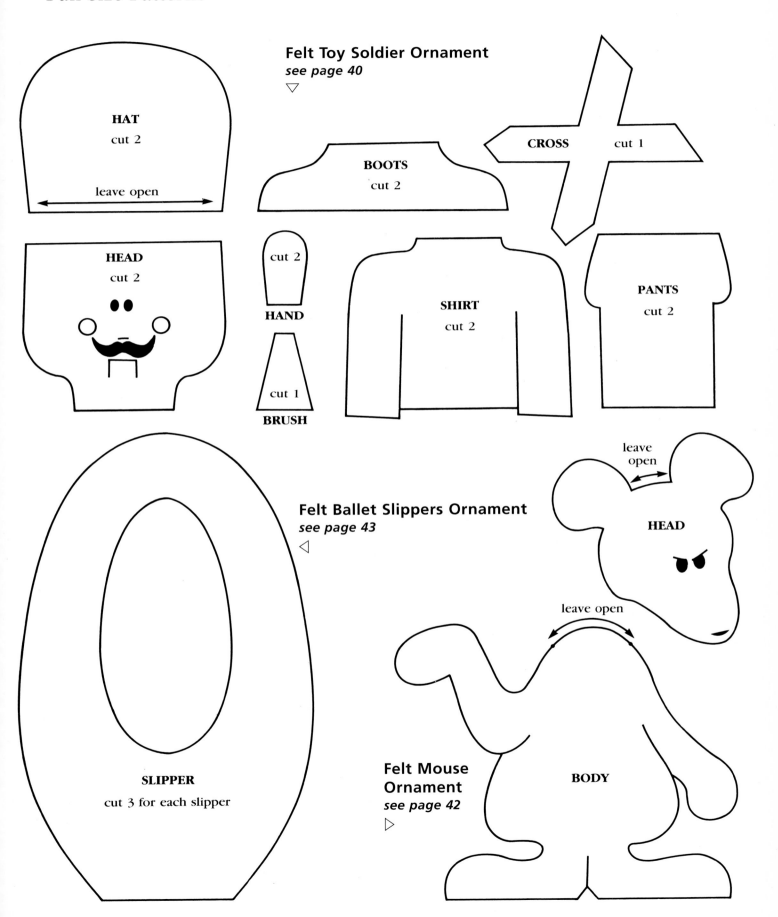

Felt Toy Soldier Ornament
see page 40
▽

HAT
cut 2

leave open

HEAD
cut 2

BOOTS
cut 2

CROSS   cut 1

cut 2
HAND

SHIRT
cut 2

PANTS
cut 2

cut 1
BRUSH

Felt Ballet Slippers Ornament
see page 43
◁

SLIPPER
cut 3 for each slipper

leave open

HEAD

leave open

Felt Mouse Ornament
see page 42
▷

BODY

Full-Size Patterns

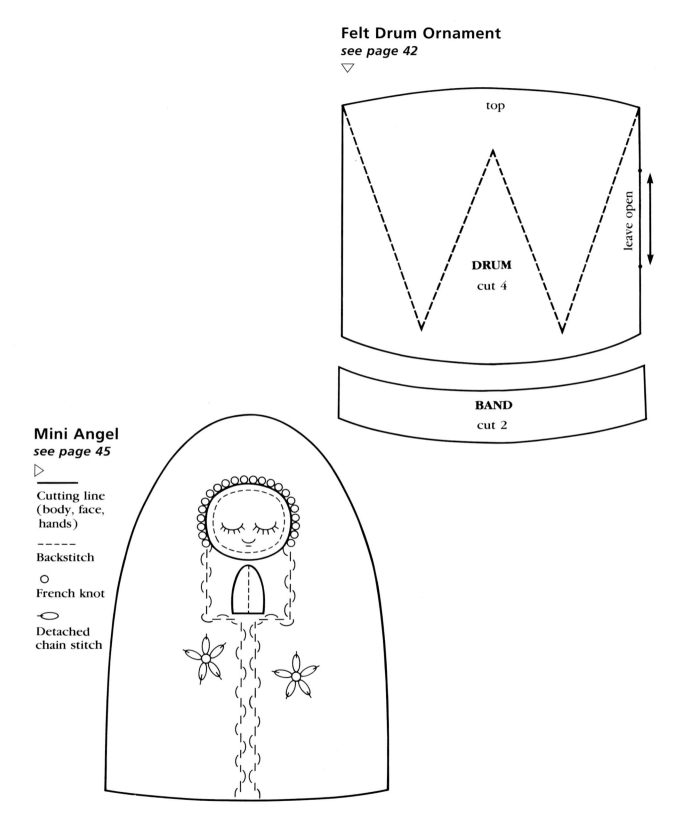

Felt Drum Ornament
see page 42

top

leave open

DRUM

cut 4

BAND

cut 2

Mini Angel
see page 45

Cutting line
(body, face,
hands)

Backstitch

O
French knot

Detached
chain stitch

Full-Size Patterns

Mr. and Mrs. Claus
see page 103

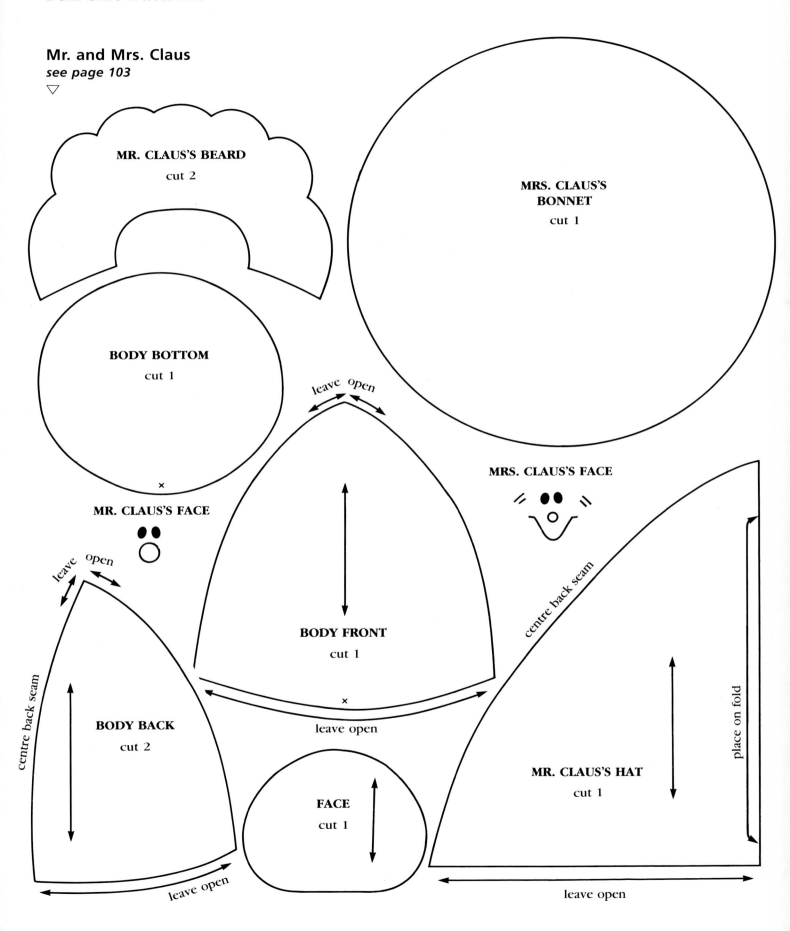

MR. CLAUS'S BEARD
cut 2

MRS. CLAUS'S
BONNET
cut 1

BODY BOTTOM
cut 1

leave open

MRS. CLAUS'S FACE

MR. CLAUS'S FACE

leave open

centre back seam

BODY FRONT
cut 1

centre back seam

place on fold

BODY BACK
cut 2

leave open

FACE
cut 1

MR. CLAUS'S HAT
cut 1

leave open

leave open

Full-Size Patterns

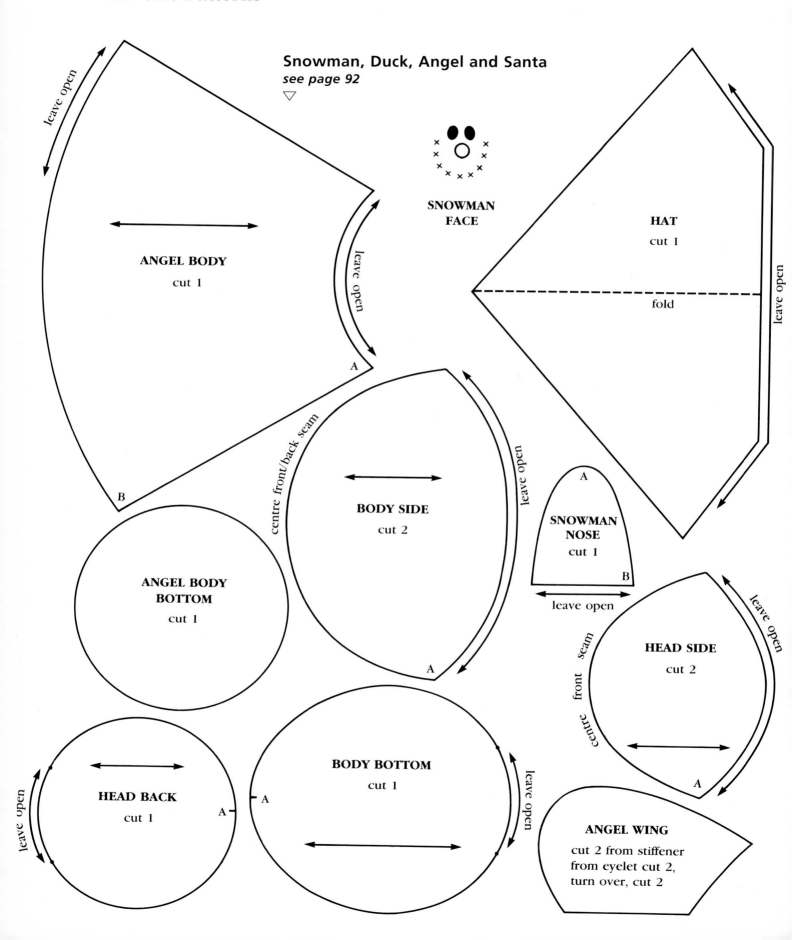

Snowman, Duck, Angel and Santa
see page 92
▽

leave open

ANGEL BODY

cut 1

leave open

A

B

**SNOWMAN
FACE**

HAT

cut 1

fold

leave open

centre front/back seam

BODY SIDE

cut 2

leave open

A

A

**SNOWMAN
NOSE**

cut 1

B

leave open

**ANGEL BODY
BOTTOM**

cut 1

centre front seam

leave open

HEAD SIDE

cut 2

A

leave open

HEAD BACK

cut 1

A

A

BODY BOTTOM

cut 1

leave open

ANGEL WING

cut 2 from stiffener
from eyelet cut 2,
turn over, cut 2

Full-Size Patterns

Snowman, Duck, Angel and Santa
continued from previous page

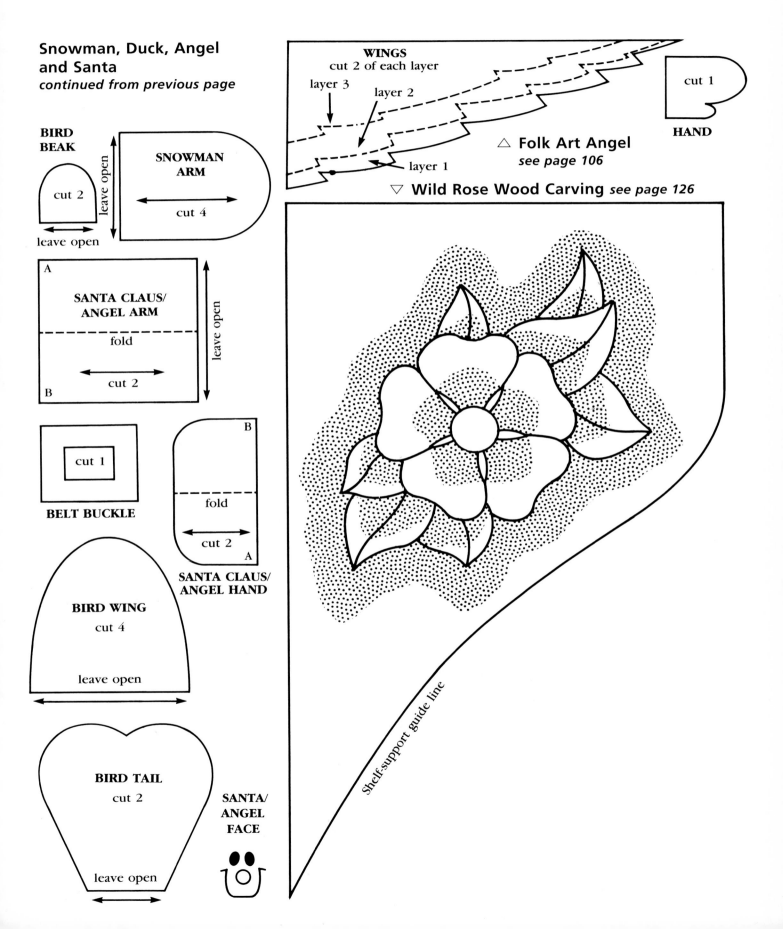

BIRD BEAK
leave open
cut 2
leave open

SNOWMAN ARM
cut 4
leave open

A

SANTA CLAUS/ ANGEL ARM
fold
cut 2
leave open

B

BELT BUCKLE
cut 1

B

SANTA CLAUS/ ANGEL HAND
fold
cut 2

A

BIRD WING
cut 4
leave open

BIRD TAIL
cut 2
leave open

SANTA/ ANGEL FACE

WINGS
cut 2 of each layer
layer 3
layer 2
layer 1

△ **Folk Art Angel**
see page 106

HAND
cut 1

▽ **Wild Rose Wood Carving** *see page 126*

Shelf-support guide line

Pattern Pieces

Santa with Attitude
see page 105

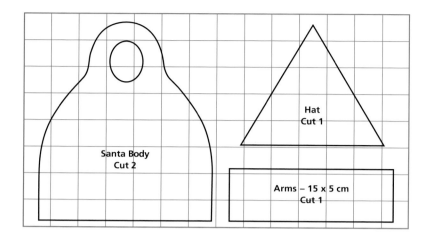

Paws
see page 110

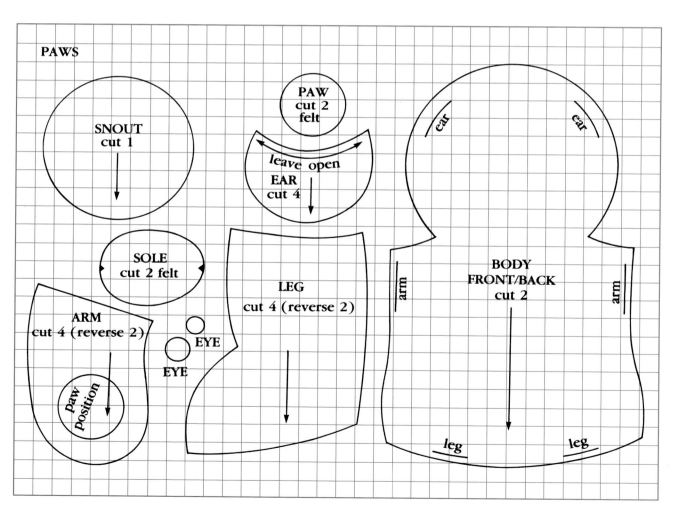

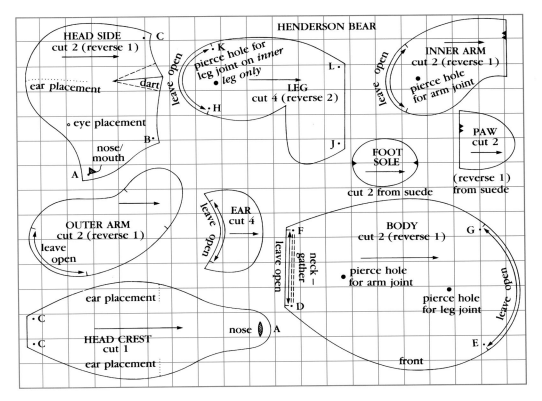

HENDERSON BEAR

HEAD SIDE
cut 2 (reverse 1)

ear placement

•K
pierce hole for
leg joint on *inner*
leg only

LEG
cut 4 (reverse 2)

•H

leave open

L •

• eye placement

nose/
mouth

B•

A•

INNER ARM
cut 2 (reverse 1)

pierce hole
for arm joint

leave open

J •

PAW
cut 2

FOOT
SOLE

(reverse 1)
from suede

cut 2 from suede

OUTER ARM
cut 2 (reverse 1)

leave
open

EAR
cut 4

leave open

BODY
cut 2 (reverse 1)

G •

F •

neck –
gather

leave open

pierce hole
for arm joint

leave open

ear placement

nose

• A

pierce hole
for leg joint

•C

•D

•C

HEAD CREST
cut 1

ear placement

E •

front

Henderson Bear
see page 112
◁

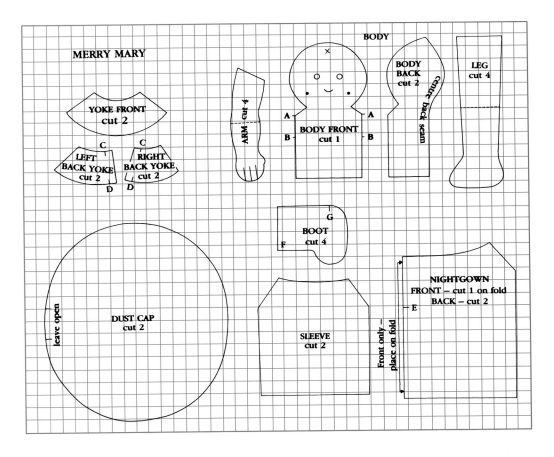

MERRY MARY

YOKE FRONT
cut 2

C   C

LEFT
BACK YOKE
cut 2

RIGHT
BACK YOKE
cut 2

D   D

ARM
cut 4

BODY

×

BODY FRONT
cut 1

A

A

B

B

BODY
BACK
cut 2

Centre back seam

LEG
cut 4

leave open

DUST CAP
cut 2

G

BOOT
cut 4

F

SLEEVE
cut 2

Front only –
place on fold

NIGHTGOWN
FRONT – cut 1 on fold
BACK – cut 2

E

Merry Mary
see page 114
◁

Acknowledgements

A special thank you to Carol Moore, Penny Nicholson, Jean Scobie-Parker, Renée Schwarz and Alisa Wing — all talented craftspeople who recreated many of the projects in unbelievable time, making it possible to meet our press deadline.

John Stephens, photographer extraordinaire, who not only photographed the new designs and brought the original ones into the digital age, but turned all of our photo shoots into a fun experience.

My gratitude to the enthusiastic and supportive staff at Madison Press Books, who believed that twenty years later this book would appeal to a new generation of crafters.
— A. H.

Photography Credits

Photography Credits

All photographs are by John Stephens except as noted:

Christopher Campbell: page 113
Greg Eligh: pages 30, 31
Frank Grant: pages 16, 18, 107 (bottom), 111, 115

Index

Index

Index

Design and Art Direction:
Silke Braun
Diana Sullada

Editorial:
Beth Martin

Production:
Kelvin Kong
Susan Barrable

Color Separation, Printing and Binding:
Lotus Printing, China